ST. COLUMBA AND IONA

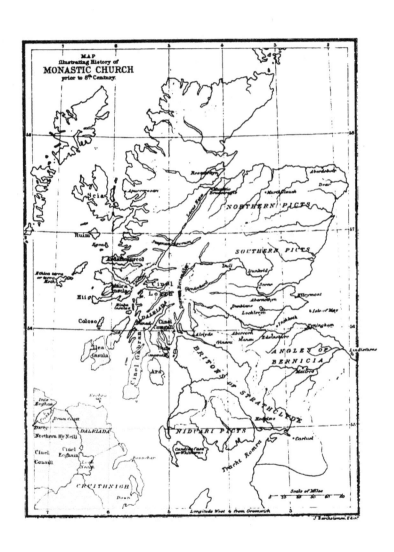

MAP
illustrating History of
MONASTIC CHURCH
prior to 8ᵗʰ Century.

ST. COLUMBA

and

IONA

*The Early History
of the Christian Church
in Scotland*

ALPHONS BELLESHEIM

Eremitical Press

SURREY, BRITISH COLUMBIA

St. Columba and Iona:
The Early History of the Christian Church in Scotland

Abridged from the *History of the Catholic Church in Scotland*
from the Dawn of Christianity to the Present Day, Volume 1

Alphons Bellesheim (1839–1912)

Translated by David Oswald Hunter Blair (1853–1939)

Copyright © 1887 Alphons Bellesheim

This paper is acid free and meets all ANSI standards
for archival quality paper.

ISBN 978-1-926777-24-5

CONTENTS

THE EARLY MISSIONARIES
(A.D. 400–563)

The First Christians in Britain

The most ancient traditions respecting the introduction of Christianity into Britain stretch back to the first century of the Christian era. It is true that the conjecture of Venantius Fortunatus that the Apostle St. Paul visited our shores has no historical foundation; for it may be taken for granted that between the periods of his first and second captivity at Rome the Apostle of the Gentiles penetrated only as far as the "western limits" of Europe—that is, in all probability, to Spain. At the same time it cannot be doubted that, even as early as the first century after Christ, there were adherents of the Christian religion in Britain. Among the Roman legions which occupied the country, there would naturally be found a certain number of Christians; and it may well be conceived that the fervor which animated these early professors of the faith would be largely instrumental in gaining fresh adherents to their creed among the natives. Recent archaeological researches have indeed conclusively proved that the Christians, not only as to numbers, but also with regard to their social position, were of considerable mark at this period in the metropolis of Britain. Prominent among them was Pomponia Graecina, wife of the proconsul Plautius, who led the Roman eagles into Britain. This lady, whose identity with St. Lucina has been practically demonstrated by De Rossi,[1] was accused, we are told, of having embraced Christianity; for we can refer to nothing else the statement of Tacitus that a charge of "foreign superstition" was brought against her. Pomponia was tried by her husband, in presence of her kinsmen, but was acquitted. The historian relates that she afterward led a life of the strictest retirement for forty years; and she appears during the reign of Claudius not only to have suffered no molestation on account of her faith, but to have been held in high esteem. It would seem that some of her kindred were likewise Christian; for De Rossi has discovered in the sepulcher of St. Lucina, in the Catacomb of St. Callisto, an epitaph recording the name of one of her relations. Claudia, the wife of Pudens, who is mentioned by St. Paul in his Epistle to Timothy,[2] is supposed also to have been of British origin. These few facts are sufficient testimony to the existence of a Christian community in Britain at a very early period.

As to the country now known as Scotland, the arms and civilization of Rome had not of course penetrated into the northern parts of our island as they had done in the south. We have, however, the evidence of Tertullian, writing at the close of the second century, that portions of Britain which the Romans had never reached were by that time "subject to Christ." Whether these words have reference to Scotland or not we have no means of ascertaining. The story first told in definite shape by Fordun, and amplified by Boece,[3] of Pope Victor sending Mark and Dionysius as missionaries to the north, at the instance of

---

1. Giovanni Battista de Rossi, *Roma Sotteranea*, vol. 2, p. 361.

2. 2 Timothy 4:20.

3. Some important sources for medieval Scottish history are the *Chronica Gentis Scotorum* by John of Fordun, the *Scotichronicon* by Walter Bower, and the *Scotorum Historia* by Hector Boece.

Donald, King of Scotland, although unquestionably based on very ancient tradition, belongs rather to the domain of legend than of solid history.

At whatever date Christianity was introduced into Britain, it seems to have enjoyed a long period of peace, which was not disturbed until the outbreak of the Diocletian persecution in 303. In pursuance of the edicts of the emperors Diocletian and Maximian, the churches were plundered and destroyed, and the Christians were compelled to seek shelter from their persecutors in the mountainous districts of the west. Among the illustrious martyrs of this time we find the names of Aaron and Julius, citizens of Caerlyon, and St. Alban. To the latter was afterward dedicated the great Benedictine abbey of St. Alban's, which preserved the martyr's relics in a magnificent shrine. In 314, a few years after the Diocletian persecution, two British bishops, Eborius of York and Restitutus of London, were present at the Council of Arles.

St. Ninian

The first authentic personage that meets us in the succession of Scottish missionaries is St. Ninian. His biographer, Aelred, abbot of the Cistercian monastery of Rievaulx in Yorkshire, belongs unfortunately to a very much later period. Venerable Bede,[4] however, had long before made honorable mention of Ninian, and Alcuin had addressed to the brothers of St. Ninian at Candida Casa a beautiful letter in which he recommends himself to their prayers in the church of the holy father Ninian, illustrious for his many virtues. And in order that the saint might be mindful of him at the throne of God, he sent together with the letter a vestment of silk, to be used in the church where reposed the relics of the saint.

---

4. Venerable Bede (672/673–735), a monk of Northumbria, author of the *Ecclesiastical History of the English People.*

According to Aelred, Ninian was the son of a Pictish chieftain of Galloway, in the south-west of Scotland, and was born about 360. From his earliest youth the spirit of true piety filled his soul. He studied diligently the Holy Scriptures, and Christ's words to Peter, "You are Peter, and upon this rock I will build my Church," made a deep and lasting impression on his mind. Arrived at adolescence, and desirous of advancing in knowledge and in the service of God, he set out through Britain and Gaul for the metropolis of the Christian world, where the holy Pope Damasus (366–384) then occupied the apostolic chair. Rome at that time still glittered with the splendor of the magnificent edifices with which she had been embellished by imperial pomp. The ancient palaces, baths, forums, statues, and theaters, and the aqueducts stretching for miles across the Campagna, had not yet been demolished by the iron hand of Alaric and his barbarous hordes. Amid these relics of paganism appeared the champions of the Christian faith—a Jerome, an Ambrose, and a Damasus. The latter was a native of Rome. Part of his life had been passed in the days of persecution. He had heard as a boy the acts of the martyrs from the very lips of the executioner, and had faithfully served the Church successively as stenograph, lector, deacon, and priest. It was he, too, who as Pope composed those noble epitaphs which still stand forth amid the ruins of fifteen centuries, and charm all who read them.

The holy Pontiff welcomed with joy the zealous Scottish youth. He assigned to him teachers to instruct him in the Sacred Scriptures and the doctrine of the Church. The progress which Ninian made was surprising, and in a short time he found himself in a position to be able to communicate to others from the stores of his own overflowing knowledge. "A worthy reward," observes Aelred, "that he who for love of truth had sacrificed country, riches, and pleasure should be led into the very sanctuary of truth, and receive for carnal goods spiritual, for earthly heavenly, for temporal eternal." Here, from the well of apostolic tradition, he drew that pure Catholic learning which he was afterward called to promulgate in his own country. Like other students of the time, too, he would visit the tombs of the Apostles and martyrs, especially the Catacombs, and pray at those venerated spots. Under Pope Siricius, the successor of Damasus, Ninian continued his studies in Rome. But when the Pontiff learned that many of the inhabitants of western Scotland had not yet received the faith, and that others had had the Gospel preached to them by heretics or by men insufficiently instructed, he bestowed upon Ninian episcopal consecration and sent him as missionary to his native country.

In obedience to the Pope's commission, Ninian departed for Britain, journeying through Gaul, where he visited St. Martin of Tours. The scene of his apostolic labors was the kingdom of Strathclyde in the south-west of Scotland, which was bounded on the north by the river Clyde, while its southern limit extended, according to the fortunes of war, to the Solway Firth, or as far as the river Mersey. Ninian employed masons whom he had brought from the renowned abbey of Marmoutier in France to erect in this district the first stone church in Scotland. On account of the white color of the material employed, it became known as Candida Casa, Whithern, or Whitehouse. According to Bede, Ninian received the news of the death of St. Martin while the building was in progress, and so deeply was he convinced of the sanctity of the holy bishop that he dedicated his new church to his memory. It was completed probably in the year 402, since that appears to have been the year of Martin's decease. Aelred describes it, situated on a promontory surrounded on three sides by the sea, and connected with the mainland only on the north. "This description," writes Mgr. Campbell, "may apply to the Isle of Whithorn, where the ruins of a chapel of unknown date are still to be seen, but may equally apply to the entire peninsula of Wigtown; and the 'Candida Casa' of St. Ninian would be the town of Whithorn, some miles inland, where the cathedral of Galloway, beautiful in its ruins, still recalls the memory of Scotland's first apostle."

The apostolic labors of St. Ninian extended beyond the district of Galloway, north of the Firth of Forth, as far as the country south of the Grampians, inhabited by the southern Picts, who under his influence abandoned their idolatrous worship and embraced Christianity. He ordained bishops and priests, and divided the country into districts, to each of which he appointed missionaries. He commenced, moreover, the erection of the so-called "Great Monastery" (*magnum monasterium*) which arose at Candida Casa on the model of the mother-house (*majus monasterium*) of Marmoutier, and in course of time developed into a celebrated training school of monks and missionaries. It was from hence that St. Cairnach, "Bishop and Abbot of the House of Martin," crossed over into Ulster shortly before Finnian of Clonard from St. David's in Wales, and introduced monasticism into the south of Ireland. The seed was thus sown which was destined to spring up a century later in the person of the renowned Columba, apostle of the northern Picts. Whithorn was visited by innumerable pilgrims from Ireland, many of whom made it for a considerable time their home. Among them are mentioned St. Finnian of Moville, who devoted himself there to the study of the Sacred Scriptures and to the rules of the monastic life; St. Enda, famous for his island school at Arann; and St. Rioch, a relative of St. Patrick. St. Manchan, patron of Limerick and one of the brightest ornaments of the Irish Church, was also a monk in St. Ninian's monastery, and St. Mugint composed there his sublime penitential prayer, which was used for centuries in the Irish Church and is preserved in the Book of Hymns.

Like most of the early Celtic saints, Ninian practiced great austerities. He is related, during the whole of Lent, to have tasted only the poorest fare, and from Holy Thursday to Easter Day to have abstained altogether from food. Like his great model St. Martin, he loved to withdraw himself from time to time from the turmoil of the world in order to devote himself more perfectly to the contemplation of heavenly things. The cave is still pointed out on the coast of Wigtownshire, whither he was accustomed to retire. It is situated high up in a precipitous range of rocks, against which the waves of the Irish Sea dash their spray.

The majority of Scottish historians place St. Ninian's death in the year 432—some on the authority of Bede, others on that of Aelred, although no such date is to be found in either writer, nor can it now be ascertained with any certainty. He was interred in his own church of St. Martin, where his mortal remains were placed in a stone sarcophagus beside the altar. His memory was preserved in the numerous churches dedicated to him, whose number Dr. Forbes estimates at not less than sixty-three.[5] The ancient Scottish liturgy celebrated his festival on September 16, while the Irish commemorate him under the name of Monennio. According to a very ancient tradition, preserved in the Festology of St. Angus, Ninian is said to have visited Ireland a few years before his death to aid in the missionary labors of St. Palladius, and to have erected at Cluain Conaire, now Cloncurry, in the county of Kildare, a chapel and monastery which reproduced in miniature his great foundation in Scotland.

As time went on, the fabric erected by St. Ninian fell into decay, but it arose again in the first half of the eighth century, when the Angles conquered the British kingdom of Strathclyde. Bede tells us that Pecthelm was the first bishop of the newly restored diocese. Up to the year 790 the bishops of Candida Casa succeeded one another in regular order. Simeon of Durham mentions that Bishop Acca was expelled from the see in 732 and died in 741. In 764 Bishop Frithwald died and was succeeded by

---

5. Alexander Penrose Forbes, *Lives of St. Ninian and St. Kentigern.*

Pecthwine and Aethelbyet. With Badulf, who was consecrated in 790, the line of bishops of English origin comes to an end. Between the years 875 and 883, Cardulf, Bishop of Lindisfarne, and Cadred, Bishop of Carlisle, embarked from the Derwent, intending to carry the relics of St. Cuthbert to Ireland, but were driven by a storm on Whithorn. A hundred years later, in 970, Kenneth II conquered Galloway and came to venerate the relics of St. Ninian. In the year 1034 Galloway became part of the kingdom of Scotland, and a new bishopric was afterward erected there through the instrumentality of David I (1124–1153). As Galloway, however, had hitherto been governed by Scottish princes, but under Saxon rule, and had been considered as an integral part of the kingdom of Northumbria, the royal founder gave his consent that the new diocese should be subject to the Archbishop of York as Metropolitan. Thenceforward the bishopric continued to exist until the Reformation: it was, however, separated from York by Sixtus IV, and constituted part of the newly formed province of St. Andrews. Finally, in 1491, it was subjected to the archiepiscopal see of Glasgow.

St. Ninian has always, as one of the first missionaries of the faith to Scotland, been held in high honor among her people. In the fifteenth century (1473) we read that Queen Margaret, accompanied by six ladies of her Court, made a pilgrimage to Candida Casa. In 1506 the Regent Albany guaranteed a safe conduct to all pilgrims who should come from England, Ireland, or the Isle of Man to Scotland, by land or by water, to the tomb of the holy Confessor Ninian. James IV, one of the most illustrious of Scottish kings, who died the death of a hero at Flodden in 1513, made eight journeys to Candida Casa. Some of the relics of the saint were saved during the storms of the Reformation and were preserved in the Scottish College at Douai. It was an arm of the saint that was taken thither, by the instrumentality of an ecclesiastic named Alexander Macquarry, the Countess of

Linlithgow, and Alexander Seton, a Jesuit. Nothing is known of Macquarry except his name. Seton was a natural son of the Earl of Dunfermline; he entered the Society of Jesus in 1687 and lived to extreme old age. The Countess of Linlithgow is well known for her faithful adherence to the Catholic religion, and as having been entrusted with the education of the Princess Elizabeth, daughter of James I, and afterward wife of the Elector Palatine of the Rhine. She and her husband acquitted themselves so well of the office entrusted to them that the King and Privy Council expressed to them their complete satisfaction. The Anglican denomination in Scotland also showed their respect for St. Ninian's memory by inserting his name in their ecclesiastical calendar in 1637.

One example may here be given of the language of respect, and even veneration, in which historians of our day have spoken of St. Ninian. "No one," writes the late Dr. Forbes, Anglican Bishop of Brechin, "can stand within the precincts of the ruined priory of Whitherne, or look out to sea from the roofless chapel of the Isle, without emotions which are difficult to describe. He stands on a spot where the ancient civilization of Rome, and the more ancient barbarism of the Meatae, alike gave place to the higher training of the Gospel of Christ—where the domination of the earth, transferred to the true faith, but still proceeding from the Eternal City, laid hold upon the strongest of all those Celtic races which constitute the population of Scotland—where Irish learning established the great monastery, and Irish piety received illustration in Brignat and Modwenna, Manceimus, Eugenius, Tighernach, and Endeus—where a Saxon Church, remarkable for the sanctity of its bishops, repaired the breaches caused by conquest and foreign oppression—where, amid the ravages of the Normans and the feuds of the local princes, a rest was found for the ashes of St. Cuthbert—where, in the great restoration of the twelfth century, the civilizing influence of the see of York, and spiritual grace of the Order of Prémontré, brought some alleviation to the barbarism of the times—where an Italian legate, mediating between the conflicting claims of Scotland and England, brought his Italian astuteness and Italian tact to bear upon the question—where Aelred acquired the knowledge which gives local color to his narrative—where the bishop of the diocese, so poor that he needed to act as suffragan and coadjutor to the Archbishop of York, yet appeared in his true place as intercessor for the rebel Thomas to his offended King—where David, wounded in battle, found a cure for his festering sore—where year by year the concourse of devout pilgrims to St. Ninian's shrine was so great as to call for royal interference, and in the presence of his sanctity the old feuds of Scots and English were for the time to be forgotten—where the good Queen Margaret, the wife of James III, found food for a piety which has almost entitled her to a place in the Calendar of the Saints—where the gallant and chivalrous James IV, in whom, in spite of the temptations of youth, the devotional element prevailed, drew in that spiritual life which, expressing itself in deep penitence for his complicity in his father's death, sent him with an iron girdle of penance round his waist to the fatal field of Flodden.

"And all this historic interest centers round one single figure, sketched in faint outline by the Venerable Bede, filled in by the graceful hand of the amiable Aelred, commemorated in the dedication of many churches through the length and breadth of Scotland—Ninian, the apostle of the Britons and of the southern Picts."

St. Palladius

The current tradition of Scottish Church history of this period points to St. Palladius as the successor of St. Ninian in the work of the conversion of Scotland. Around this name has gathered a literature of its own. Who were the Scots, to whom he received his mission from the Pope? Did he in truth ever tread the soil of that country which is known today as Scotland? Where did he meet his death? Can St. Servan be identified as his disciple? These are questions which have received various answers according to the standpoint of different historians; and for their now almost complete solution we have to thank the careful, but at the same time reverential, researches of Dr. William Forbes Skene,[6] whom we shall here follow as a trustworthy guide.

Let us see first what are our sources of information. Prosper of Aquitaine tells us that in the year 429 Agricola the Pelagian, son of the Pelagian Bishop Severianus, had caused his heresy to be introduced into Britain. The orthodox clergy acquainted the Bishops of Gaul with this fact, and the latter in consequence summoned a synod, which determined to send Germanus, Bishop of Auxerre, and Lupus, Bishop of Troy, into Britain, to recall the wanderers to the Church. It was at the instance of the deacon Palladius that Pope Celestine entrusted this mission to Germanus. Prosper assigns the year 431 as the date when the same Pope bestowed upon Palladius episcopal consecration and sent him to the Scottish Christians as their first bishop. "And when ordained Bishop for the Scots," he goes on, "while he aimed at preserving the Roman part of the island in the Catholic faith, he converted the barbarian portion also to Christianity." The information thus given us by a writer who was contemporary with Palladius does not exclude the possibility of Christianity having been introduced into Ireland before this date, but it renders it probable that Ninian, if he ever visited Ireland at all, was by this time dead. We learn from it the existence of a British Church, which extended northward as far as the northern Picts and westward to Ireland. It must not be forgotten that Ireland was the only country at that time inhabited by the people called Scots. "We find," says Skene, "this Church in close connection with that of

6.   William F. Skene, *Celtic Scotland.*

Gaul, and regarding the Patriarch of Rome as the head of the Western Church and the source of ecclesiastical authority and mission; and with the exception of the temporary prevalence of the Pelagian heresy in Britain, we can discover no trace of any divergence between them in doctrine or practice."

In course of time we find these traditions assuming quite another form. "In the year 430," writes Fordun in the fourteenth century, "Pope Celestinus sent Saint Palladius into Scotia, as the first bishop therein. It is therefore fitting that the Scots should diligently keep his festival and Church commemorations; for by his word and example, he with anxious care taught their nation—that of the Scots, to wit—the orthodox faith, although they had for a long time previously believed in Christ. Before his arrival, the Scots had as teachers of the faith and administrators of the Sacraments priests only, or monks, following the rite of the primitive Church. So he arrived in Scotland with a great company of clergy, in the eleventh year of the reign of King Eugenius; and the king freely gave him a place of abode where he wanted one. Moreover, Palladius had as his fellow worker in preaching and administering the Sacraments a most holy man, Servanus, who was ordained bishop, and created by Palladius his coadjutor—one worthy of him in all respects—in order to teach the people the orthodox faith, and with anxious care perfect the work of the Gospel; for Palladius was not equal to discharging alone the pastoral duties over so great a nation." Of St. Terrenanus, another of Palladius's disciples, Fordun writes: "The holy bishop Terranan likewise was a disciple of the blessed Palladius, who was his godfather, and his fostering teacher and furtherer in all the rudiments of letters and of the faith."

This statement of Fordun, or rather the version of the ancient traditions which he here presents to us, has been hitherto received by historians without further question. But a closer examination will render it very doubtful whether Palladius was ever in Scotland, and will probably make it necessary to place St. Servanus at a very much later period.

The only authentic information on the subject which we possess, besides the Chronicle of St. Prosper, is contained in the various Lives of St. Patrick. The oldest of these are found in the Book of Armagh. In the annotations of Tirechan, it is stated that Palladius, "as the ancient saints relate, suffered martyrdom among the Scots" (that is, the Irish). Muirchu in his Life of St. Patrick writes of the apostolate of Palladius in Ireland: "Neither did those rude and savage people readily receive his doctrine, nor did he wish to pass his time in a land not his own. But returning hence to him who sent him, having begun his passage the first tide, little of his journey being accomplished, he died in the territory of the Britons." In the Life of St. Patrick by Mark the Hermit, appended to the *Historia Britonum* of Nennius, it is related that Palladius was prevented by storms from landing in Ireland. "For no one can receive anything on earth except it be given him from above. Returning therefore from Ireland to Britain, Palladius died in the land of the Picts." The Life of St. Patrick, which Colgan calls the third, states that Palladius returned to go to Rome but died in the land of the Britons. Other authorities, however, relate him to have suffered martyrdom in Ireland. According to the Tripartite Life, a sickness seized him in the country of the Cruithne, of which he died. On comparing these statements, we find Ireland in the first place assigned to Palladius as the theater of his labors; but for Ireland is afterward substituted Britain. The story told by Mark the Anchorite of his being prevented from landing by a storm receives a further development later on. In the Scholia attached to the Hymn on St. Patrick quoted by Colgan, and attributed to Fiech of Sletty, we are told that Palladius founded three churches in Ireland. "Nevertheless he was not well received by the people, but was forced to go round the coast of Ireland toward the north, until, driven by a great tempest, he reached the extreme part of the Modhaid toward the south, where he founded the churches of Fordun and Pledi." Another biographer transfers his martyrdom altogether from Ireland and places it at Fordun in the Mearns, on the east coast of Scotland between Montrose and Aberdeen.

The latter form of the legend, which takes him round Scotland and lands him on the east coast, in the district of the Mearns, is undoubtedly to be traced to the fact that this church of Fordun possessed the relics of the saint. According to the Aberdeen Breviary, they were brought thither by his disciple Terrananus, who is said to have received from Palladius baptism and instruction in the faith, and to have died and been buried at Banchory-Ternan. Now, if we take together the two facts that Angus the Culdee, in his metrical Calendar, speaks of "Torannan, the long-famed voyager over the broad shipful sea," and that the ancient scholiast on this Calendar says that "Torannan the far-famed voyager—that is, Palladius—was sent from the successor of Peter to Erin before Patrick: he was not received in Erin, whereupon he went to Alban, and is buried in Liconium," (probably the old name of Banchory-Ternan)—we have the key to enable us to understand the statements that Palladius was the apostle of the Scots. This connection with Scotland consists only in the fact that Terranus, or Ternan, brought his relics, either from Ireland or from Galloway, to his home at Mearns, in the territory of the southern Picts.

The foregoing solution of the difficulties connected with the life of St. Palladius cannot, owing to the obscurity in which that period is involved and the scarceness of contemporary documents, be considered as absolutely satisfactory and conclusive. It is not in fact possible to arrive at the truth of the matter with perfect certainty. And since an ancient and venerable tradition points to St. Palladius as an apostle of Scotland, Leo XIII was fully justified, in his bull restoring the Scottish hierarchy in 1878, in accepting the Devotion tradition in question and reviving, as it were anew, the veneration due to St. Palladius. We meet with this, indeed, in every century. In the Aberdeen Breviary he is commemorated on July 6, and the Arbuthnot Missal contains a hymn which celebrates the apostolic labors of St. Palladius. St. Ternan died at Banchory, on the Dee, in the east of Scotland. Here his relics were preserved until the Reformation, among them his famous bell and his magnificently bound copy of the Gospels. The Church celebrated his feast on June 12, with a proper Office and Mass.

St. Servanus

Besides Terrananus, Servanus or St. Serf is also mentioned by Fordun as a disciple of Palladius. We read further, in a fragment of an ancient Life of St. Kentigern, that "on his arrival in Scotia, Palladius found St. Servanus there, and called him to work in the vineyard of the Lord of Sabaoth; and when afterward the latter was sufficiently imbued with the teaching of the Church, Palladius appointed him his suffragan over all the nation of the Scots." The same Life mentions as Kentigern's birthplace Culross, where he was educated by Servanus, and where he died in 603, in extreme old age. This connection between Kentigern, whose life extended into the seventh century, and Servanus, whom Palladius was said to have found in Scotland in 430, might be admitted as possible, supposing that both lived to a great age. There is extant, however, a very ancient Life of Servanus, which says nothing of the saint having been the disciple of Palladius and the teacher of Kentigern, but brings him into connection with Adamnan, the famous Abbot of Iona and authentic biographer of St. Columba. According to this Life, Servanus founded the church of Culross in the reign of Brude, king of the Picts (697–706). "It is obvious, therefore," remarks Skene, "that there is a great anachronism in placing this Servanus as the instructor

21

of Kentigern, and that he in reality belongs to the century after his death. We are thus left with Terrananus or Ternan alone, as having any claim to belong to this period, and the dedications to him show that the field of his labors was the territory of the southern Picts, who are said by Bede to have been converted some time before by Ninian."

The Picts and the Scots

The chronicles of the Picts clearly indicate a connection at this period between the Church of the southern Picts and that of Ireland which was founded by St. Patrick, the successor of Palladius. Nectan, king of the Picts from 458 to 482, founded the church of Abernethy in honor of St. Bridget. Nectan had visited the great Irish saint at Kildare when he was driven from his kingdom and had taken refuge in Ireland, and she had prophesied to him the restoration of his throne. It is recorded of Boethius, or Buitte, founder of the church of Mainister Buitte in Ireland, that he arrived in the country of the Picts with fifty followers and restored to life King Nectan, who was just dead. Upon a site granted him by the king he built a church, near Dunnichen (anciently known as Duin Nechtain). An MS. Life of St. Buitte, preserved in the Bodleian Library, gives the county of Londonderry as his birthplace. Even in childhood he possessed an astonishing knowledge of the Sacred Scriptures. To perfect himself in learning he proceeded to Italy, where he lived for several years in a monastery. He brought back with him from Rome many precious relics and copies of the Gospels. The church of Inchmocholmoc (now Inchmahome), in the Loch of Menteith, was dedicated to St. Mocholmoc (or Colman), who founded his monastery of Dromore certainly before 514. The parish of St. Fillan's, on Loch Earn, takes its name from Fillan, an Irish monk; and the church of Aberdour, on the Firth of Forth, is also dedicated to him.

Early in the sixth century, we find the first beginnings of Christianity in the Scottish kingdom of Dalriada. Here, north of the river Clyde and westward from the mountain range of Drumalban, in the present county of Argyll, three Irish chieftains, Fergus Mor, Lorn, and Angus, sons of Erc, who had themselves already embraced Christianity, established the little kingdom which was destined in the middle of the ninth century, under the valiant Kenneth MacAlpine, to absorb the neighboring states and to become the foundation of the kingdom of Scotland. They came from the district of Dalriada, in Ulster, which St. Patrick is recorded to have visited, and where he is said to have founded several churches. On visiting it a second time, in order to confirm the people in the faith, he is said to have found the twelve sons of Erc in possession of the sovereignty, and to have prophesied of one of them, Fergus, that he should be a king and should reign over the Picts. Up to the second half of the sixth century, when they came into conflict with Brude, king of the northern Picts, the Dalriadic people appear to have continually extended their sway, embracing within it the Western Islands, including Iona and Mull. Lorn, Fergus, and Angus were buried in Iona. "There appears," says Skene, "to have been in the island of Iona, even at this early period, a Christian establishment of that peculiar collegiate form which appears at this time in Ireland, for Angus the Culdee invokes in his Litany the seven bishops of Hy, or Ia." One of the most celebrated missionaries of Scottish Dalriada was St. Modan, who, according to Adam King, died in 507.[7] The ruins of Balmodhan—that is, St. Modan's Town—on Loch Etive, near the spot where afterward arose the priory of Ardchattan, mark the site of St. Modan's first oratory.

If we cross the Clyde and turn to the district church of Scottish Dalriada, we find a mixed population of Britons, Picts, and Saxons, the majority of whom professed Christianity, and, like

7.   Adam King, *Kalendars.*

Dalriada, were in close connection with the Irish Church. This is strikingly exemplified in the legend of St. Monenna, of which three versions are extant. According to one of these, she was an Irish nun, who sent one of the sisters of her convent, named Brignat, to Rosnat (a name by which Candida Casa or Whithern was known). In another version she is said to have founded seven churches in Scotland, one of them at Dunedene, "which in Anglic is termed Edeneburg." She died in 519. Monenna is probably identical with the holy virgin Medana or Edana, commemorated in the Aberdeen Breviary on November 19. "Edinburgh," writes Cardinal Moran, "is commonly supposed to have been so called from a fort erected there by King Edwin; but long before that monarch's time, St. Edana's sanctuary there was a place of pilgrimage. One of the most interesting places connected with this saint is her cave chapel, situated close to the Mull of Galloway, in the parish which from her derives its name, Kirkmaiden or Maidenkirk."

Such are the scanty notices which are all that have come down to us regarding the earliest period of the Church in Scotland. Much as this fact is to be regretted, no blame is attributable in the matter to the Church or to her bishops. It is to be referred far more to the wholesale pillage and senseless destruction of an immense number of documents bearing on Church history at the time of the schism of the sixteenth century. On this point Father Thomas Innes, who was one of the first since the Reformation to direct the attention of Scottish scholars to the ancient Church, writes as follows: "The registers of the churches and bibliotheques or libraries were cast into the fire; and these were so entirely destroyed that if in Scotland there had happened a debate about the consecrations or ordinations of bishops and priests, either before or about the time of the Reformation, I do not believe that of all our ancient bishops and priests, ordained within the country, there could have been found the register or act of consecration of any one of them—so careful were our first Reformers to sweep clean away all that could renew the memory of the religion in which they had been baptized. . . . At St. Andrews, the metropolitan church, besides the archives where all the records and rights of the Church, such as bulls of popes, charters of the kings, all ecclesiastical Acts, such as those of national councils, of diocesan synods, of processes in the ecclesiastical courts . . . consecration of bishops, all ordinations, dispensations, etc., were preserved. Since the time of the Reformation all these original records have no less entirely and universally disappeared (excepting some of the chartularies) than if they had never been."[8]

Toward the middle of the sixth century, the Church had obtained a footing among the Scots of Dalriada in the present county of Argyll, the southern Picts living north of the Firth of Forth as far as the Grampians, and the mixed tribes of Britons, Picts, and Saxons south of the Firths of Forth and Clyde. The light of the Gospel had not yet reached the northern Picts. Nor indeed, even in the districts just mentioned, does Christianity appear to have everywhere taken deep root, for evidence is extant which points to a relapse into paganism. In the letter of St. Patrick to the subjects of the tyrant Coroticus, the ancestor of the princes of Strathclyde (written, according to Haddan and Stubbs, about the year 492), the saint in feeling and vivid language deplores the vices of the Picts, whom he openly charges with apostasy; and he is not more indulgent to the evil deeds of Coroticus himself, on whom he calls down the severest judgments of God. Jocelyn, the biographer of St. Kentigern, is probably reporting a perfectly genuine tradition when he states that the Picts, who had received the faith from the preaching of St. Ninian, had relapsed into paganism. So, too, an older Life of St. Kentigern terms one of

---

8. Thomas Innes, *A Critical Essay on the Ancient Inhabitants of the Northern Parts of Britain or Scotland.*

the Pictish princes of Lothian "a semi-pagan." Such statements as these leave no room for doubt that, in the course of hardly half a century, the Christian faith had been to some extent overthrown by the revival of paganism. In order to rescue it, there was need of an institution resting upon a solid basis, which should take up the well-meant but unproductive endeavors of the secular clergy, concentrate them in the strict discipline of the monastic life, and impart to them at the same time a stronger impulse and a more enduring efficacy. The Scottish Church enters now, under the influence of the Irish monks, on the monastic period of her history, which lasted until the middle of the ninth century, when it gave way to the Culdees, who were succeeded in their turn, about the middle of the eleventh century, by the ordinary constitution of the Church.

ST. COLUMBA (A.D. 521–597)

The Irish Church

The character of the second or monastic period of the Scottish Church can only be fully understood by first glancing at the development of the Irish Church, with which the Church in Scotland was at this time very closely connected, and whose impress she in large measure received.

Usher published, from MSS. of the eighth century, a "Catalogue of the Saints of Ireland according to their different periods," and we find also in the Leabhar Breac, and in the Book of Leinster, the Litany of Angus the Culdee, in which he invokes the saints of the early Church in different groups. "The first order of Catholic saints," says the Catalogue, "was in the time of Patrick; and then they were all bishops, famous and holy, and full of the Holy Spirit—three hundred and fifty in number, founders of churches. They had one head, Christ, and one chief, Patrick; they observed one mass, one divine office, one tonsure from ear to ear. They kept one Easter, on the fourteenth moon after the vernal equinox; and what was excommunicated by one church, all excommunicated. They rejected not the services and society of woman. The second order was of Catholic priests.

For in this order there were few bishops and many priests, in number three hundred. They had one head, our Lord: they celebrated different masses, and had different rules: one Easter, on the fourteenth moon after the equinox; one tonsure from ear to ear: they refused the services of women, separating them from the monasteries. This order has lasted for four reigns [to 572]. The third order of saints was of this sort. They were holy priests, and a few bishops, one hundred in number, who dwelt in desert places, and lived on herbs and water, and the alms; they shunned private property, and despised all earthly things; they had different rules and masses, and different tonsures, for some had the corona, and others the hair behind, and a different time for observing Easter. For some celebrated the Resurrection on the fourteenth moon, others on the sixteenth. These lived during four reigns, and continued to the great mortality" (in the year 666). This passage enables us to trace three distinct periods in the development of the Irish Church: in the first, we find a secular clergy; in the second, a regular or monastic clergy; in the third, an eremitical clergy.

The differences which characterized the early Church during these successive periods originated, as Skene rightly observes, to great extent in the social state of the people. It would therefore be a fatal error to infer from such accidental modifications any radical change in the constitution of the Church. On the contrary, this was carefully preserved, even when unable for a time to attain in all directions to its full development and authority. "The distinction in order," remarks Skene, "between bishop and presbyter seems to have been preserved throughout, though their relation to each other, in respect to numbers and jurisdiction, varied at different periods." The period of St. Patrick may be termed the episcopal period: the saints of this epoch regarded Patrick as their leader or chief. The latter, in his *Confession*, states merely that he ordained clerics, but in the Catalogue of the Saints we read that "they were all bishops, three hundred and fifty in number, founders of churches." And Angus the Culdee, in his Litany, invokes "seven times fifty holy bishops, and three hundred priests whom Patrick ordained." We may infer from this that Patrick placed a bishop in every church which he founded. These prelates were known as *chorepiscapi*, and their great number will surprise us less when we remember that we meet with a similar state of things at that time in other Churches, especially in Asia Minor. The great number of Irish bishops, however, was the necessary consequence of the so-called *Tuath* or tribal system. Each tribe represented a living organization, and would as such desire to have a bishop, in order that the ecclesiastical might correspond with the civil constitution. Wherever Patrick could obtain the grant of a site from a chieftain, there he built churches, and seems to have placed in each *Tuath* or tribe a bishop, under whom were several priests. The Episcopate was in this way founded on a system of race and tribe, and bore the character of a federal union; and it is to this that the words seem to refer, "what was excommunicated by one church was excommunicated by all." No trace is to be found of any metropolitan jurisdiction, although Patrick, as founder of the Church, was during his life reverenced as its head, as he distinctly implies himself in his epistle to Coroticus. "All the bishops," says the Catalogue of the Saints, "were sprung from the Romans and Franks and Britons and Scots." By the Romans and Britons are to be understood those who followed Patrick from Britain to Ireland, while the Franks were probably of Gaulish origin. It is evident that the foreign element predominated at that period in the Irish Episcopate.

We are told of the first order of the saints of the Irish Church, that "they rejected not the services and society of women," or, according to another MS., that "they excluded from their churches neither laymen nor women," which indicates that they belonged to the secular, in contradistinction to the regular or monastic clergy. They kept Easter on the fourteenth moon after the vernal equinox—that is, from the fourteenth to the twenty-first day of the month, according to the reckoning of the Roman Church, with which the Irish Church was in agreement until the year 457. Their tonsure, as opposed to the Pauline, which included the whole head, and to the Petrine, in which a corona of hair was left, extended "from ear to ear," the forepart of the head only being shaved, and the hair at the back of the head being allowed to grow.

The system of St. Patrick underwent a modification toward the end of his life, in the establishment of collegiate churches, consisting of seven bishops. This new institution was in still closer connection with the *Tuath* or tribal system, inasmuch as the bishops in question were usually taken from one and the same family. Tirechan mentions that Patrick passed the Shannon three times, and completed seven years in the western quarter, and came from the plain of Tochuir to Dulo Ocheni, and founded seven churches there. And again, "The seven sons of Doath—that is, Cluain, Findglais, and Imsruth, Culcais, Deruthmar, Culcais, and Cennlocho—faithfully made offerings to God and St. Patrick." Angus the Culdee gives a list of no fewer than a hundred and fifty-three such groups of seven bishops.

The second period of the Irish Church is marked by its distinctly monastic character. Monachism was introduced into Ireland from two sources. The first of these was Whithern, in Galloway, where dwelt Ninian, the friend and disciple of St. Martin of Tours. In the legend of St. Cairnech, St. Ninian's monastery is termed the "house of Martain." According to the same legend, Cairnech crossed from Whithern into Ireland, where he became "the first bishop of the Clan Neall and of Teamhar, and the first martyr and the first monk of Erin." Other missionaries soon followed in his footsteps. We learn from the Lives of St. Tighernac of Clones and St. Eugenius of Ardistraw, both natives of Leinster but connected with Ulster families on the mother's side, that they were carried off in their youth to Britain by pirates, with a number of other boys. The king, at the queen's intercession, sent them to a holy man named Monennus, or Nennio (Ninian), to be educated in his monastery of Alba. They afterward returned to Ireland and received episcopal consecration. Tighernac founded the monasteries of Galloon and Clones. So, too, we read in the Acts of St. Enda, that his sister sent him to the monastery of Rosnat (Whithern) in Britain, where he became the disciple of St. Mancenus. And St. Monenna sent one of her relatives, named Brignat, to the same monastery, to be instructed in the rules of monastic life. St. Finnian, too, or Finnbar, of Moville, went in boyhood to St. Caelan, Abbot of Noendrum, who placed him under the care of the holy bishop Nennio. By him he was taken to Britain and trained for a number of years in the "*Magnum Monasterium.*" He afterward founded the monastery of Magh Bile or Moville, in Down. Mugint wrote his Hymn or Prayer, as he tells us in his preface, in the monastery of Futerna. We have evidence here of the intimate connection that existed at this period between Ireland and Scotland, for the names of Rosnat, Futerna, and *Magnum Monasterium* signify alike the monastery of St. Ninian at Candida Casa.

Besides the monastery of St. Ninian, the second great channel through which monachism reached Ireland was by way of Brittany and Wales. When Tours, in the year 394, became the civil and ecclesiastical capital of the province of Lugdunensis Tertia, the metropolitan see of St. Martin embraced the southern provinces of Maine and Anjou, and extended northward as far as Brittany. Under St. Martin's influence, monasticism was soon introduced into Brittany, where the monasteries of Landouart and Landevenech were founded; and from thence it passed into Wales. The Catalogue of the Saints states that those of the second (or monastic) order "received a mass from Bishop David, and Gillas and Docus the Britons." Bishop David is, of course, the celebrated founder of the church of Menevia, now St. David's; Gillas, or Gildas, is the well-known historian of the sixth century; and Docus is St. Cadoc, who founded the great monastery of Llancarvan in South Wales, where Gildas was associated with him. From Wales monasticism passed St. Finnian into Ireland through St. Finnian of Clonard. He received his early education from Fortchern of Trim and Caiman of Dairinis, an island in the Bay of Wexford. At the age of thirty he crossed over to Kilmuine in Wales, where he found the three holy men, David, Cathmael (or Cadoc), and Gildas, and became their disciple. For thirty years he remained in different monasteries in Wales, and then returned with many followers to Ireland, "to gather together a people acceptable to the Lord." Here he founded the famous monastery of Cluain-Erard, or Clunard, afterward a great training school for Irish missionaries. This vast establishment, situated on the Boyne Water in Meath, is said to have contained three thousand monks. Animated by a desire to visit Rome, Finnian set out on the road to Italy. But an angel of God appeared to him, with the words, "What would be given to you in Rome, shall be given to you here. Arise, and renew sound doctrine after the example of St. Patrick." The same fact is narrated also in the Office of St. Finnian, where he is said to have been persuaded by an angel to return to Ireland, to restore the faith which had fallen into neglect.

St. Columba in Ireland

These expressions indicate clearly that the Church, which since the death of St. Patrick had fallen into decay, was now to be revived and reinvigorated through the foundation of a number of important monastic centers. Among the great Irish monasteries which came into existence at this period, one of the principal is that founded by St. Columba at Derry in 545. An old Irish account thus narrates the foundation: "Columcille (Columba) went to Daire—that is, to the royal fort of Aedh, son of Ainmire, who was king of Erin at that time. The king offered the fort to Columcille; but he refused it, because of Mobhi's command. On his coming out of the fort, however, he met two of Mobhi's people bringing him Mobhi's girdle, with his consent that Columcille should accept a grant of territory, Mobhi having died. Columcille then settled in the fort of Aedh and founded a church there." Ainmire, the father of Aedh, and Columba were cousins—hence the important gift here mentioned is intelligible enough: the saint was thus enabled by his kinsman's help to commence his illustrious career as abbot and founder of monasteries. Columba established besides the church of Raphoe, and the famous monastery of Durrow, in the diocese of Meath. Bede terms it a "noble monastery, which, from the profusion of oak trees, is called in Scottish Dearmach, or the plain of oaks."

Besides these, his principal monasteries in Ireland, he is said to have founded many others, as Cennanus, or Kells, in the county of Meath, which, according to the old Irish Life, was formerly a fort of Diarmada, son of Cerbaill. "Columcille marked out the city in extent as it now is, and blessed it all, and said that it would become the most illustrious possession he should have in the land." Dr Reeves gives a complete list of St. Columba's Irish foundations.

Of at least equal importance with the foregoing was the great monastery of Bangor in Ireland, founded by St. Comgall in 558. Such was the attraction of his reputation for sanctity and learning that three thousand monks, dwelling in different cells and monasteries, were under his care. The renown of this institution was still great in the time of St. Bernard of Clairvaux, who in his Life of St. Malachy makes honorable mention of the monastery of Bangor and the numberless houses that sprang from it. In testimony of the blessing of God which attended their labors, he mentions the monk Luanus, who is said to have been the founder of no fewer than a hundred monasteries in Ireland and Scotland. Angus the Culdee invokes "forty thousand monks under the rule of Comgall of Bangor." Skene, however, supposes this number to have been written for four thousand in the original text.

Irish monasteries

When we hear of so astonishing a number of character Irish monasteries at this period, we must not think of magnificent buildings such as are associated with the noble abbeys of the middle ages. The ancient Irish monastery consisted of a row of small cells, constructed not of stone but of wood or osier-work. When Columba visited the monastery of Mobhi Clairenach, on the banks of the river Finglass, he found there fifty monks dwelling in huts on the western side of the river, east of which rose the *Ecclais*, or church. When Ciaran of Saighir, one of the twelve apostles of Ireland, was erecting the huts of his monastery, he employed the rudest materials, which a wild boar assisted him to collect by tearing off branches with its tusks. It is related of St. Monenna that she built a monastery of smooth planks according to the fashion of the Scottish nations, who were not then accustomed to construct walls of stone. When St. Finan, who had been a monk of Iona, was chosen Bishop of Lindisfarne, he erected there a cathedral church, built, as Bede records, in the Irish fashion, not of stone, but entirely of hewn oak, with an outer covering of reeds to protect it from the weather. St. Paulinus, Archbishop of York, is said to have visited the famous church of Glastonbury, constructed of wreathed osiers, and to have covered it with wood and lead. The name given to the ancient Irish church of wood was *Duirthech*, from *dairthech*, a house of oak; or *Deirthech*, from *dear*, a tear—that is, a house in which tears are shed. It was not until the end of the eighth century that the devastations of the Danes caused the churches to be constructed of more solid materials. For the same reason they were provided with towers or belfries, which, in case of Danish incursions, might serve as places of security for the monks as well as for the treasures of the Church.

The number of inmates of these monastic buildings varied considerably. We find some containing a hundred and fifty monks, while in others they amounted to several thousands. Thus the monastery founded by Enda in the island of Aran possessed a hundred and fifty monks; and Angus the Culdee, in his Litany, invokes "thrice fifty true monks under the rule of Bishop Ibar," "thrice fifty true monks under the rule of Munnu, son of Tulchan," "thrice fifty true monks in the grace of God at Dairiu Chonaid." In connection with Mochuda he invokes no less than "seven hundred true monks, who were buried at Rathinn," and again "eight hundred who settled with Mochuda in Lismore." Then there is the important monastery of Lethglin, where he invokes "the three hundred and twelve hundred monks, who sang the praises of God under Molaisse, the two Ernas, and the holy martyr-bishops of Lethglin." Finally, the celebrated monastery of Clonard, the training school of the twelve apostles of Ireland, contained, as we have said, three thousand monks.

Whether so great a number of persons could actually find shelter within the enclosure of a single monastery may appear doubtful. The numberless offshoots and dependent houses were probably considered as included under one and the same establishment. All were united to one another by ties of fraternal affection, and felt themselves to be members of one family. This bore the name of *Muintir*, a term which was used to designate as well the inmates of each separate monastery as the mother-house with its dependencies. The monks were called brethren, and the head of the monastery was the abbot. The seniors, who were well instructed in sacred science, occupied themselves chiefly in copying the Holy Scriptures. Under Bishop Mochta, in the monastery of Lugmagh, there were sixty such seniors, of whom it is said in the Donegal Martyrology:

> Threescore psalm-singing seniors
> Were his household, royal the number;
> Without work, except reading.

A particular class of brethren, the lay-brothers, were occupied in manual labor; while others again undertook the education of the alumni, or pupils of the monastery.

Such institutions as we have described did much not only for the propagation of religion and the cultivation of learning, but also for the social advancement of the people. "The monastic system," says Skene, speaking on this point, "which thus characterized the Irish Church in its second period, and pervaded its organization in every part, forming its very life, presented features which peculiarly adapted it to the tribal constitution of the social system of the Irish, and led to their being leavened with Christianity to an extent which no other form of the Church could have effected. These large monasteries, as in their external aspect they appeared to be, were in reality Christian colonies, into which converts, after being tonsured, were brought under the name of monks. Thus we are told in the Life of Brendan, that as soon as he had been ordained priest by Bishop Ere, 'He also received from him the monastic garb; and many leaving the world came to him, whom he made monks; and he then founded in his own proper region cells and monasteries,' till they reached the number of three thousand. There was thus in each tribe a Christian community to which the people were readily drawn, and in which they found themselves possessed of advantages and privileges, without their actual social position with reference to the tribe and the land being essentially altered. They formed, as it were, a great ecclesiastical family within the tribe, to which its members were drawn by the attractions it presented to them.

These were, first, greater security of life and property. Before the tribes were to any extent brought under the civilizing influences of Christianity, life must have been, in a great measure, a reign of violence, in which every man had to protect his life and property as he best might; and the struggle among these small communities, either to maintain their own rights or to encroach on those of others, and the constant mutual warfare to which it gave rise, must have exposed the lives of their members to incessant danger. To them the Christian community offered an asylum in which there was comparative rest and relief from danger at the cost of observing the monastic rule."

The state of Ireland in the time of Columba is graphically illustrated in an anecdote of his early life, told us by Adamnan. "When the holy man," he says, "while yet a youth in deacon's orders was living in the region of Leinster, learning the divine wisdom, it happened one day that an unfeeling and pitiless oppressor of the innocent was pursuing a young girl who fled before him on a level plain. As she chanced to observe the aged Gemman, master of the foresaid young deacon, reading on the plain, she ran straight to him as fast as she could. Being alarmed at such an unexpected occurrence, he called on Columba, who was reading at some distance, that both together, to the best of their ability, might defend the girl from her pursuer; but he immediately came up, and without any regard to their presence, stabbed the girl with his lance under their very cloaks and, leaving her lying dead at their feet, turned to go away back. Then the old man, in great affliction, turning to Columba, said, 'How long, holy youth Columba, shall God, the just Judge, allow this horrid crime and this insult to us to go unpunished?' Then the saint at once pronounced this sentence on the perpetrator of the deed: 'At the very instant the soul of this girl whom he has murdered ascends into heaven, shall the soul of the murderer go down into hell.' And scarcely had he spoken the words when the murderer of the innocent, like Ananias before Peter, fell down dead upon the spot before the eyes of the holy youth. The news of this terrible and sudden vengeance was soon spread abroad throughout many districts of Ireland, and with it the wonderful fame of the holy deacon." Adamnan's Life of Columba furnishes a number of similar instances, illustrating clearly the insecure state of the country.

These Christian communities early enjoyed the privilege of sanctuary—a privilege which, founded as it is in great measure upon divine law and natural right, it would be a misapprehension to look upon, as Skene appears to do, as a mere fiction of human invention. We find it recognized among the Irish at a very early period. When Diarmaid, King of Ireland, was defeated by Hy-Neill at the battle of Culdremhne in 561, the popular voice attributed his ill fortune to the fact of his having killed Curnan while under the protection of Columcille. The same Diarmaid violated the sanctuary of Ruadhan of Lothra, one of the twelve apostles of Ireland, and carried off by force to his fortress at Tara a person under Ruadhan's guardianship. By refusing to give him up, Diarmaid drew upon himself the curse of Ruadhan. For, "Roadanus and a bishop that was with him took the bells that they had, and cursed the king and place, and prayed God that no king or queen ever after should dwell in Tarach, and that it should be waste forever, without court or palace, as it fell out accordingly"—or as an old Irish poem has it—"From the judgment of Ruadhan on his house, there was no king at Teamraigh or Tara."

The system which regulated the succession of abbots in the Irish monasteries was one of somewhat peculiar character. While the Church in other respects held firmly to the principle of the propagation of her priesthood by spiritual succession, and avoided accordingly, in the bestowal of benefices, whatever might appear to favor hereditary claims, we find nevertheless, in consequence of the peculiar state of society in Ireland, with which monasticism was very closely connected, that the successors to the abbatial dignity were chosen from among the kindred of the founder of the abbey. The publication of the Brehon laws has given us some insight into this system.

The erection of a monastery might come about in one of two ways. Either the king granted a *Rath* or fortified place, for the purpose, or else the chief of a tribe, generally that to which the founder himself belonged, gave a site and land on which to erect the abbey. Private property, in the strictest sense of the word, was unknown in Ireland at this time. The right of possession was in fact vested not in the individual, but in the tribe. If the founder belonged to the same tribe as the bestower of the grant, the monastery was looked upon as so far the property of this family or tribe, that when the abbacy fell vacant it was filled by the appointment of a member of the family. There existed thus, to use the words of Reeves, a "*plebilis progenies*," or lay family, from which were chosen the *Co-arbs*, or successors of the first abbot, who formed the "*Ecclesiastica progenies*," and who, being unmarried, was without lineal successors. Failing a descendant in direct line from the founder, one was selected from a collateral branch of the family. At the foundation of the monastery of Derry by St. Columba, it so happened that the tribe of the granter of the land was the same as that of the founder, and Columba was consequently succeeded by his kinsmen. If, on the other hand, the granter belonged to a different tribe, the successors to the abbacy were usually, though not always, appointed from the family of the founder of the monastery. Such a right, however, was only recognized when a suitable person was available from the family in question, "even though he should be but a psalm-singer." We have an instance of this in the monastery of Drumcliffe, which Columba founded in the territory of a stranger tribe. In the old Irish Life of the Saint he is said to have given "the authority and the clergy and the succession to the Cinel Conaill forever"—that is, to his own tribe.

We thus find in Ireland a connection between Church and people even closer than that existing in Continental countries. There arose from this relation a number of reciprocal rights and duties, by which the Church and society in Ireland were mutually bound. The Church claimed from the tribe the firstlings of flocks and tithes of the produce of the soil. Every tenth son also was considered as belonging to the Church. His position is thus defined: "The son who is selected has become the tenth or as the firstling to the Church; he obtains as much of the legacy of his father, after the death of his father, as every lawful son which the mother has, and he is to be on his own land outside, and he shall render the service of a free monk to the Church, and the Church shall teach him learning; for he shall obtain more of a divine legacy than of a legacy not divine." The term *Manach* or monk, here used, comprised all who were connected with the monastery, down to its lowest dependants. Even these latter were distinguished with various privileges, which must necessarily have raised the clerical status very considerably. "The enslaved," say the ancient laws, "shall be freed, the plebeians exalted through the orders of the Church and by performing penitential service to God. For the Lord is accessible: He will not refuse any kind of man after belief, among either the free or the plebeian tribes; so likewise is the Church open for every person who goes under her rule."

Side by side with the rights of the Church from the tribe we find the claims of the tribe against the Church. These are thus stated: "They demand their right from the Church—that is, baptism and communion and requiem of souls, and the offering from every Church to every person after his proper belief, with the recital of the Word of God to all who listen to it and keep it." The exact import of the second of these "rights "is not clear, but it appears to have some reference to the offering of the sacrifice of the Mass for the intention of individuals. In any case, these statements of rights afford evident proof of the close connection between Church and tribe. The position of the Irish Church during her second period is clearly indicated in the words of a contemporary tract: "It is no *Tuath* or tribe without three free *neimhedh*, or dignitaries: the *Eclais* or church; the *Flaith*, or lord; and the *File*, or poet."

It was, however, in its religious aspect that Irish monasticism exerted its principal and deepest influence on social life. The zeal of missionary enterprise was an inseparable and essential element of monasticism in Ireland at this time, as at other periods of Church history. It was from Ireland that there flowed that marvelous stream of heaven inspired men who in the adjacent islands, in Britain, Caledonia, Gaul, Germany, Switzerland, and Italy, achieved such mighty results. The shorter the space of time during which their labors extended, the more powerful the enemy which they had to encounter, the simpler the means which they employed—so much the more wonderful appears the success to which they attained. It was, in truth, not so much by the preaching of the Word as by the silent eloquence of their holy lives that the missionaries succeeded in vanquishing the abominations of paganism. The moral sublimity of their mode of life paved the way for the efficacious preaching of the Gospel. Hence the reverence of these rude children of nature for the ministers of the Church, who claimed as their sole authority their divine commission, and who assuredly did not call in the aid of superstition to enforce it, since the overthrow of paganism with its diabolical superstitions was the sacred object which as servants of the true God they had in view. It is far more reasonable to ascribe the supernatural element in their lives to the direct intervention of God, which has never been wanting when there was need of His revealing Himself to man.

St. Columba comes to Iona

It was at this time that there came forth from the ranks of the Irish monks the man whom God had destined to be the apostle first of the northern Picts, and afterward, through the beneficent influence which flowed from his monasteries, of the whole of Scotland. When we consider the marvelous work wrought by him and his fellow laborers, we cannot but endorse the words of Marianus Scotus, written in his Chronicle of the year 589: "Ireland, the island of saints, is full of holy and wonderful men." The labors of the monastic missionaries had hitherto been confined partly to the coasts and surrounding islands, partly to the southern Picts. None had as yet ventured to penetrate to the Picts of the north. Columba took upon himself this great and arduous task; and when his long life of toil drew to its close, he was to have the joy of knowing that it had been brought to a happy solution.

Columba was born at Gartan, in the county of Donegal, on the 7th of December, 521. An ancient chapel still marks the place of his birth, and in the neighboring churchyard two old Celtic crosses recall his memory, together with a well to which devout pilgrims are still wont to resort in honor of the saint. On his father's side he was sprung from the kingly house of the northern Hy-Neill: his father, Fedleimidth, was a scion of the family of Cinell Conaill, and consequently allied to the kings of Dalriada. His mother, Eithne, belonged to the princely house of Leinster. Columba, a child of promise, was baptized by the priest Circuithnechan, and received the name of Colum, to which the word Cille (or church) was added in token of his zeal and diligence in the service of God. According to a beautiful legend, God bestowed on the youth as he grew up the gifts of virginity, wisdom, and prophecy.

Arrived at early manhood, Columba sought the schools of Moville, Clonard, and Glasnevin. At Moville his teacher was the renowned Finnian, who, according to the Donegal Martyrology, predicted to him that he was destined by the fame of his piety, and the luster of his pure life, his purity, wisdom, learning, and eloquence, to astonish the whole Western world. In the monastery of Glasnevin, near Dublin, he studied under St. Mobhi, and among his fellow students was St. Ciaran, the future Abbot of Clonmacnoise. A destructive war which broke out in the district dissolved the convent of Glasnevin in 544, and Columba returned to the north of Ireland. Mobhi died in 545, and in 546, as already mentioned, Columba, when just twenty-five years of age, founded the monastery of Derry. In the year 549 Columba lost his famous master, St. Finnian. About 553 he established the great monastery of Durrow, his principal work in Ireland. With regard to the remaining Columban foundations in Ireland, their precise dates cannot now be ascertained, but they fall in the period from 546 to 562, when the saint crossed into Caledonia.

In the year 561 was fought the battle of Cooldreony, in which Columba appears to have taken part, at least indirectly. The circumstances which follow are related by Manus O'Donnell in his biography of the saint which appeared in 1532.

At Cuil Dremhne, in the province of Connaught, not far from the borders of Ulster, a fierce battle took place in 561. The contending parties were Diarmaid, son of Cerbaill, chief of the southern Hy-Neills and King of Ireland, and the northern Hy-Neills with other princes and the people of Connaught under their king Aedh. The King of Ireland was defeated with great loss. The occasion of the contest was twofold. In the first place, King Diarmaid had violently removed Curnan, son of the King of Connaught, from Columba's care; and secondly had, in a dispute pending between Columba and Finnian of Moville, given his judgment against Columba. The dispute in question related to a copy of the Psalter which Columba had made against the will of Finnian, the legitimate owner, and which Finnian claimed as his property. Columba, who belonged to the northern branch of the Hy-Neills, was said to have incited the members of his clan to war against the King of Ireland, and to have contributed by his prayers to the success of their arms. A synod of the Irish saints afterward assembled and held Columba accountable for the blood that had been shed. In expiation of his fault, he was charged with the task of rescuing from paganism precisely as many souls as the number of Christians that had fallen in that battle. Laisren of Inishmurray was intrusted with the carrying out of this sentence. He imposed upon Columba the penalty of perpetual banishment: his eyes were never again to look on Ireland, his feet were never again to tread her soil. Forthwith Columba left his home, and turned his steps toward the Western Isles. He landed first upon the island of Colonsay; but when, on climbing its highest peak, he found that Ireland was still in sight, he would not remain there. He betook himself to the island of Iona, from whence his gaze could no longer discern his native land. Here he resolved to take up his abode and to erect a monastery. So runs the popular tradition.

With regard to Columba, we are in a position to be able to investigate the facts by means of a biography which can lay claim in the highest degree to historic truth, since it depends upon contemporary records, and was compiled by a successor of Columba in office scarcely a hundred years after his death. Adamnan twice refers to the celebrated battle, and both times certainly in connection with Columba's departure to Scotland. He also mentions that Columba was excommunicated by a synod at Taillte, in Meath; that Columba presented himself at this assembly, and that when St. Brendan of Birr perceived him, he bowed before him respectfully and embraced him. When reproached for this behavior, he rejoined that he had remarked certain signs accompanying the appearance of Columba, which convinced him that the latter was marked out by God to be the guide of His people. Thereupon not only was the excommunication withdrawn, but Columba was treated with the greatest respect. Adamnan does not connect this ecclesiastical assembly with the battle mentioned above; he merely remarks that Columba had been excommunicated for some trifling reason, and, as afterward appeared, unjustly. This does not, however, exclude the possibility that these reasons, of which he makes no more definite mention, afforded a pretext, if only a remote one, for the battle in question. The story of the contest having been brought about by the pretended acquisition of a copy of the Psalter, against Finnian's will, has a very improbable sound, when we remember the good understanding between those illustrious men, as repeatedly attested by Adamnan. The violation of the right of sanctuary, on the contrary, of which King Diarmaid had been guilty toward Columba, called, according to the Irish standard of right at that period, for the strongest reprobation. On one side the rights of the Church, on the other the honor of a princely family, were at stake, and it appeared that the sword alone could decide between them. To what extent Columba may have exercised influence on his kinsmen can never now be accurately known.

The remaining part of the tradition, however, according to which Columba was forced into exile by the synod of Taillte, must be rejected entirely. Adamnan does not mention a word of it, although he had the greater reason to do so that the penalty of banishment undoubtedly marked a turning point in the life of the hero of his biography. Adamnan does not attribute the resolution of Columba to leave his home to any external influence, least of all to any cause derogatory to the saint. He recognizes only his boundless love of God, which led him to abandon his home and to go as a missionary to Caledonia. Similarly the ancient Irish Life of Columba tells us that "the illustrious saint left his home for the love and favor of Christ," with the further addition that "this was the resolution which he had determined on from the beginning of his life"; and this view is confirmed by the statement of Bede. We have a remarkable testimony to the spirit of meekness which filled Columba, from the lips of his contemporary Dalian Forghaill. According to him he was "a perfect sage, believing in Christ, learned, and chaste, and charitable; he was noble, he was gentle, the physician of the heart of every sage, a shelter to the naked, a consolation to the poor: there went not from the world one who was more constant in the remembrance of the cross." Angus the Culdee, in his Calendar of the Saints, speaks of St. Columba as one "who from his tenderest years cherished the most ardent love of Christ." And the portrait of Columba's character drawn by Adamnan leaves on the reader the impression that vindictiveness was very remote indeed from the nature of the saint.

Before Columba departed to Caledonia on his missionary labors, he betook himself to Inishmurray, in Sligo, on the west coast of Ireland, in order to take counsel with the Bishop Molaise, who dwelt on this island with his monks. The memory of that period is still recalled to us by the wonderfully preserved monastic cells, resembling those of a beehive, over which the storms of thirteen centuries have swept. The bishop encouraged him to carry out his design, and set before him its marvelous results. In the year 563 Columba set sail thence for Caledonia, accompanied by twelve companions, among whom was Mochenna, the son of an Ulster chieftain. In vain Columba sought to persuade him to devote his services to his native Ireland. "You," answered the inspired missionary, "are my father, the Church is my mother, and my country is wherever I can win souls for Christ."

Columba chose as his place of settlement the island of Hy, or Iona, generally known as Hy-Columbkille—the island, that is, of Columba—a part of the Scottish kingdom of Dalriada. The landing was effected on Whitsunday, the 12th of May 562. It is probable that the settlement was preceded by an invitation from the prince of Dalriada, who was allied to Columba by ties of kindred. The island formed at that time the boundary between the Dalriadan Picts on one side, and the northern Picts on the other, and must in consequence have had a peculiar attraction for St. Columba as a central point for his missionary labors. On the eastern side of the island soon arose the cells of the monks, constructed of wood and earth, while on slightly elevated ground was erected the *Tuguriolum*, or abbot's cell. Such were the obscure and insignificant beginnings of an institute which was destined in the course of time to bestow upon millions of men the benefits of religion, culture, and civilization. Only with feelings of the deepest wonder and emotion have men, even those in whose ideas of religion the spirit of monasticism was incompatible with true Christianity, visited this venerated spot. "We were now treading," wrote Dr. Johnson a century ago, "that illustrious island whence savage clans and roving barbarians derived the benefits of knowledge and the blessings of religion. . . . Far from me and from my friends be such frigid philosophy as may conduct us indifferent and unmoved over any ground which has been dignified by wisdom, bravery, or virtue. That man is little to be envied whose patriotism would not gain force upon the plain of Marathon, or whose piety would not grow warmer among the ruins of Iona!"

Similar sentiments of emotion are expressed by the learned Chalmers in his *Caledonia*. "Saint Columba came not to destroy, but to save; not to conquer, but to civilize. His name will always be remembered as the disinterested benefactor of Scotland. . . . Let us not think lightly of the saints of Iona, who were the instructors of our fathers when they were ignorant, and the mollifiers of our progenitors while they were still ferocious. The learning—I was going to say the charity—of these ages centered all in Iona. It received the persons of living kings who retired from unstable thrones, and it equally admitted dead kings from the bloody field. From this seminary went out the teachers of the Caledonian regions. To this school the princes of Northumbria were sent, and acquired the light of the Gospel from the luminaries of Iona."

In 1870 the Duke of Argyll published his work on Iona, in which the following passage occurs: "Columba was an agent, and a principal agent, in one of the greatest events that the world has ever seen—the conversion of the northern nations. Christianity was not presented to the Picts of Caledonia in alliance with the impressive aspects of Roman civilization. The tramp of Roman legions had never been heard in the Highland glens, nor had their clans ever seen with awe the majesty and power of Roman government. In the days of Columba, whatever tidings may have reached the Picts of Argyll or of Inverness must have been tidings of Christian disaster and defeat. All the more must we be ready to believe that the man who at such a time planted Christianity successfully among them must have been a man of powerful character and of splendid gifts."

For two years Columba devoted his care to the newly founded colony of Hy. Besides the general guidance of the community, he spent some time, as was customary in the Irish monasteries, in manual labor. He employed himself also in the transcription of the text of the Sacred Scriptures; and at this occupation, which had been the favorite one of his youth, he continued to toil with untiring zeal to extreme old age. The famous Book of Kells is his work, and he is said to have transcribed three hundred copies of the Gospels. The virtues which he displayed as a man, a Christian, and a monk, spread his fame far and wide, and drew crowds of pilgrims to Hy. Columba early sought to establish friendly relations with the princes of the country. Conall, King of Dalriada, received a visit from the saint at Cindelgend, in the peninsula of Cantyre, and made him a formal grant of the island of Hy.

The religion of the northern Picts

While the Scots of Dalriada, as we have already seen, had by this time, in great part at least, embraced Christianity, the northern Picts were still plunged in paganism. In 565, two years after his landing in Iona, Columba determined to attempt their conversion. The king of the Picts at this time was Brude, son of Maclochon, rightly styled by Bede "a most powerful prince," who, after repeatedly vanquishing the Scots of Dalriada, had fixed his residence in the neighborhood of Inverness. Here Columba visited him, accompanied by two of his brethren, whose names, though not recorded in the lives of the saint, are preserved in the biography of St. Comgall. They were St. Comgall, the illustrious founder of Bangor, and St. Canice, the patron of Kilkenny. When the heathen monarch refused to receive the missionaries, Columba had recourse to prayer, upon which the gates of the palace fell to the ground. Brude, on perceiving the strangers, drew his sword to kill them; but on St. Canice making the sign of the cross, the king's hand was suddenly withered, and so remained until the day on which he received at the hands of St. Columba the sacrament of baptism. After this the king not only gave Columba full permission to preach the faith throughout his dominions, but showed himself henceforth a true friend and supporter of his missionary labors. The ancient Irish Life narrates the opposition that the saint encountered from Mailchu, a son of the king, who came with his Druid to uphold paganism; but they both perished at the prayer of Columba. Columba visited King Brude several times, and throughout his life enjoyed his friendship, which not even the repeated efforts of the Druids, the official representatives of paganism, were able to disturb. Once when the saint was chanting vespers with his companions not far from the royal residence, the Druids approached and endeavored to interrupt their devotions. Columba immediately began, in marvelously clear and powerful tones, to sing the forty-fourth Psalm, "*Eructavit cor meum verbum bonum*," "My heart is astir with a good word." His voice rang like thunder in the ears of the astonished Druids, who fled in terror from the spot. The protection of King Brude secured to Columba immunity from the smaller chieftains of the country.

Of the further labors of St. Columba among the northern Picts, Adamnan has left us only scanty details. A monarch so powerful and so influential as King Brude having been won to Christianity, it may be assumed that Columba encountered few further obstacles, at least from external sources, in his work of evangelization. One of the principal means which the saint employed was the foundation of monasteries, or small Christian colonies. From the few incidents narrated by Adamnan, we learn that he did not confine his missionary labors to the poor, but wrought conversions also among the petty chieftains of the country. In one instance, we are told that he was traveling on the shores of Loch Ness, when he heard that an ancient man, a heathen, but one "who had preserved his natural goodness through all his life even to extreme old age," was at the point of death. Hastening to the district of Airchartdan (now Glen Urquhart), he "found there an old man whose name was Emchat, who, on hearing the Word of God preached by the saint, believed and was baptized, and immediately after, full of joy, and safe from evil, and accompanied by the angels who came to meet him, passed to the Lord." On another occasion St. Columba was staying in the island of Skye, when a boat came into the harbor, at whose prow sat an old man, the chief of the Geona cohort. Two youths brought him and laid him at the feet of the saint. After being instructed in the Word of God through an interpreter, he believed and was baptized. He died immediately afterward and was buried in the same spot. Both these aged converts belonged to the class of *Flaith*, or chieftains.

Adamnan gives us but little information as to the character of the paganism which Columba and his companions had to encounter. In order to obtain any accurate knowledge on this point, it is necessary to go to Irish sources. The ancient Life of St. Patrick says that "he preached threescore years the Cross of Christ to the *Tuatha* (or tribes) of Feni. On the *Tuatha* of Erin there was darkness. The Tuatha adored the *Side*. They believed not the true Godhead of the true Trinity." What is meant by the *Side* we learn from the Book of Armagh, which relates that St. Patrick and his disciples assembled one morning at a certain well, near the palace of the kings of Connaught. "And lo, the two daughters of King Laoghaire, Ethne the Fair and Fedelm the Ruddy, came early to the well to wash, after the manner of women, and they found near the well a synod of holy bishops with Patrick. And they knew not whence they were, or in what form, or from what people, or from what country; but they supposed them to be men of *Sidhe*, or gods of the earth. And the virgins said unto them, 'Where are you, and whence come you?' And Patrick said unto them, 'It were better for you to confess to our true God than to inquire concerning our race.' The first virgin said, 'Who is God, and where is God, and of what is God, and where is His dwelling place? Has your God sons and daughters, gold and silver? Is He ever-living? Is He beautiful? Did many foster His son? Are His daughters dear and beauteous to men? Is He in heaven or on earth, in the sea, in rivers, in mountainous places, in valleys? Declare unto us the knowledge of Him. How shall He be seen? How is He to be loved? How is He to be found—in youth or in old age?'" We see from this passage that the pagan religion of the Irish was a personification of the powers of nature, which were supposed to dwell in visible things, such as earth, sea, rivers, mountains, and valleys, and had to be invoked and propitiated. This worship, indeed, was extended not only to the powers of nature themselves, but also to the objects in which they were believed to reside. Tuathal Teachmahr, a mythical Irish king, is said in the Book of Conquests to have received from his people, as a pledge that the sovereignty should ever remain in his family, "sun and moon, and every power which is in heaven and on earth." So, too, King Laogaire, the contemporary of St. Patrick, had to give, in pledge of his promise never again to attack Leinster, "sun and moon, water and air, day and night, sea and land." These forces of nature, or demons, were termed by the people *Side* or *Aes Side*. In connection with this was the class known as *Druaday* or Druids, who were supposed to be able to conciliate these gods of the earth, or to practice incantations by means of their influence with them.

The paganism which St. Columba set himself religion of to overthrow in Scotland was practically identical with the religion of the Irish Druids. An ancient poem attributed to him contains the following lines, remarkable in this connection:—

I adore not the voice of the birds,

Nor the *sreod*, nor a destiny on the earthly world,

Nor a son, nor chance, nor woman;

My *Drui* is Christ the Son of God.

Adamnan mentions that Broichan, the magician, occupied an influential position at the Court of King Brude. The term *magus*, however, is used as the equivalent of *Druadh*, and in the ancient Irish Christian MSS. the Three Holy Kings (*magi*) are in fact styled the *Druad*.

Two incidents, related by Adamnan in his Life, throw some light on the nature of the religion of the northern Picts. Columba on one occasion, when preaching in the province of the Picts, converted a peasant, who received baptism together with his whole family. A few days afterward the son of the new convert fell dangerously ill, and in a short time expired. Thereupon the *Magi*, or *Druadh*, bitterly reproached the parents for their adoption of Christianity, extolled their false gods, and spoke disdainfully of the God of the Christians as inferior to theirs in power. Columba, however, came and raised the youth from the dead, thus confirming the peasant in his faith. Again, when Columba was staying in the province of the Picts, he heard of a certain well, "famous among the heathen people, which the foolish men, having their senses blinded by the devil, worshipped as God." The saint blessed the well, and, with his companions, washed his hands and feet in it, and drank of the blessed water. "From that day," says Adamnan, "the demons departed from the fountain; and not only was it not allowed to injure anyone, but even many diseases amongst the people were cured by this same fountain." On another occasion, Broichan, the *Magus* of King Brude, threatened Columba that he would make the wind unfavorable to him and bring about a great darkness. When the saint arrived at the lake, it grew very dark and a violent wind arose, at which the *Magi* began to exult. "Nor should we wonder," says Adamnan, "that God sometimes allows them, with the aid of evil spirits, to raise tempests and agitate the sea." Columba, however, called on Christ the Lord and embarked in his small boat, which ran against the wind with extraordinary speed.

"We thus see," observes Skene, "that the paganism which characterized the Irish tribes and the nation of the northern Picts exhibits precisely the same features; and all the really ancient notices we possess of it are in entire harmony with each other in describing it as a sort of fetishism, which peopled all the objects of nature with malignant beings to whose agency its phenomena were attributed—while a class of persons named *Magi* and *Druadh* exercised great influence among the people, from a belief that they were able through their aid to practice a species of magic or witchcraft. . . . How unlike this is in every respect to the popular conception of what is called the Druidical religion will be at once apparent. The process by which this monstrous system has been evoked was simply to invest the same *Druadh* with all the attributes which Caesar and the classical writers give to the Druids of Gaul, and to transfer to these northern regions all that they tell of Druidism in Gaul."

St. Columba's later life and legacy

In the years 573 and 574, Columba lost two of his most faithful friends. St. Brendan of Birr was called to his reward in 573, and for centuries his name and memory were held in honor in the monastery of Hy. The following year died Conall of Dalriada, Columba's royal protector. He was succeeded in the kingdom by his son Aidan, who was solemnly ordained to his high office by the saint in the island of Hy. According to the law of the country, the succession should have fallen to his cousin Eogan, whom Columba would perhaps have preferred to see on the throne, had he not been warned in a vision to appoint Aidan. The latter accordingly received consecration from the saint, who prophesied during the ceremony that the throne of Dalriada would remain to Aidan, to his children and children's children. The consummation of this solemn liturgical act was the first step toward obtaining the recognition of the complete independence of the kingdom of Dalriada from the Pictish monarch. In addition to this, however, it was Columba's object to loosen, or if possible to dissolve entirely, the connection of the Scottish Dalriada with the mother country. Accordingly, in the year 577, accompanied by King Aidan, he attended a synod which had been summoned to meet at Drumceatt, on the river Roe, in Londonderry. The clergy and chieftains of Ireland assembled here in large numbers, and Dallan Forgaill, the poet-biographer of Columba, relates that the saint appeared with a numerous retinue. Accompanying him, he tells us, were "forty priests, twenty bishops, noble, worthy; for singing psalms, a practice without blame, fifty deacons, thirty students." The synod at which Columba assisted with this brilliant following was held not far from his own monastery of

Derry, and it was doubtless with the object of making as imposing an appearance as possible that he was attended by so many
bishops and priests. Three subjects appear to have occupied the
attention of the synod. The first was the release of Scannlan-
More, prince of Ossory, who had been imprisoned for refusing
to pay the customary tribute to the King of Ireland. Although
Columba did not succeed in obtaining his immediate release, he
prophesied to him his speedy liberation, and moreover, that he
was destined to rule his people for thirty years. In pledge of his
words he gave to the imprisoned prince his pastoral staff, which
he had brought from Iona, and which was afterwards preserved
as a precious relic in his monastery at Durrow. The second subject under of Scottish consideration was the independence of
the Scottish kingdom of Dalriada. As a colony or subject state
it was liable not only to pay tribute, but also to render military
service to the Irish monarch. At the instance of St. Columba,
Scottish Dalriada was declared independent, binding itself at the
same time to an offensive and defensive alliance with the mother
country, maritime expeditions being alone excepted.

The third question before the synod was one which enlisted
Columba's liveliest interest. It related to the privileges of a class of
men with whom the renown of the Irish name was very intimately
connected. The bards were not only poets and musicians; they
were also the national historians, who handed down from one
generation to another the events and achievements of the past.
From time immemorial they had enjoyed extensive privileges,
one of which, known as *conmed*, consisted in the right to exact
refection for themselves and their retinue from the tribes with
which they dwelt. The numerous abuses to which this custom gave
rise were the occasion of many complaints, which were brought
before the assembly of Drumceatt for its decision. Columba, who
was himself a poet, eloquently pleaded the cause of the bards and
besought the king's favor in their behalf. It was extended to them

on the condition that their numbers should be at once reduced; and Columba was charged with the task of drawing up rules in accordance with which their privileges were to be restricted in future. The bards expressed to their great champion an undying gratitude, and their chief poet dedicated to St. Columba the celebrated poem known as the *Amra*, or praise of Columcille. The saint, however, in his humility refused to accept the panegyric, and forbade the poet to publish it during his lifetime.

Few people cling with more tenacious love to their parent soil than the children of Ireland; and this national characteristic meets us frequently in St. Columba's life. This visit to his beloved native land stirred the deepest feelings of his soul and filled him with poetic fire. To this period, probably, belongs the poem or hymn in which he paints in a series of beautiful pictures the romantic charms of Irish scenery, with its ever-verdant hills and rocky shores, on which the surge of the waves continually breaks. "What joy," he sings, "to fly upon the white-crested sea, and to watch the waves that break upon the Irish shore! . . . Carry my blessing across the sea, carry it to the west. My heart is broken in my breast; if death comes to me soon, it will be because of the great love which I bear to the Gael." So, too, in the way in which Columba dealt with his penitents we recognize the same deep love for his native land. The most severe penance that he could award them was the prohibition ever again to set foot upon the soil of Ireland; while, on the other hand, when exhorting others to return to their country, he seemed to hesitate to pronounce the name of Erin lest he should be unable to suppress his own emotions. The monastery of Derry was in a peculiar degree the object of his affection, which he has expressed in one of his most touching poems.

Returning to Iona, Columba was now able to look back, not without thankfulness and joy, to the twelve years of untiring labor which he had spent in his island home. His monastery represented the central point of the missions which were developing on every side, and the ceaseless exertions of himself and his monks had planted among the Picts the germs of a new religious, moral, and social life, and had confirmed and kindled into fresh vitality the Christian faith of the people of Dalriada. He had won to Christianity the powerful Pictish monarch and his house, while the colony of Dalriada was secured in its political independence of Ireland. Finally, his zeal and energies had called into being a very considerable number of monastic institutions in Ireland and in Scotland, which grouped themselves round Iona as their center and did not cease to remain in close connection with her. These monasteries recognized the jurisdiction of the mother house of Iona, and their inmates formed the great organization known as the family of Iona, or *Muintir Iae*. Adamnan leaves us uncertain as to the number of these foundations and the dates of their erection. We can gather, however, from his narrative that some of them belong to the earlier period of Columba's missionary labors; and all, of course, were founded during his life in Iona.

Ireland possessed a large number of churches, either founded by St. Columba, or dedicated to his memory on account of their connection with some event of his life. Still more numerous were the monasteries and churches in Scottish Dalriada and the country of the Picts which owed their origin to the saint. The following were the principal Columban foundations among the Scots: 1. Soroby, in the island of Tiree. 2. Elachnave, one of the Garveloch islands; adjacent to which is Culbrandon—i.e., *Secessus Brendani*. 3. Loch Columcille, in Skye. 4. The island of Fladdachuain, north-west of Skye. 5. The island of Trodda, south-east of the preceding. 6. Snizort (formerly Kilcolmkill), in Skye, where are still to be seen what are described as "the ruins of a large cathedral." 7. Eilean Coluimcille, an island east of Skye. 8. Garien, in the parish of Stornoway, in Lewis. There was a chapel here called St. Colm's Church. 9. Ey, the peninsula of Ui, in Lewis. 10. St. Colm's Isle, in Loch Erisort, Lewis. 11. Bemera, a small island close to North Uist. 12. Kilcholmkill, in North Uist. 13. Kilcholambkille, in Benbecula. 14. Howmore, in South Uist. 15. St. Kilda. 16. Canna. 17. Island Columbkill, in Loch Arkeg, Invernessshire. 18. Killchallumkill, a chapel at Appin, opposite Lismore. 19. Kilcolmkill, in Ardchattan. 20. Kilcolmkill, now Morvern, in Argyllshire. 21. Kilcollumkill, in Mull. 22. Columkille, on the east coast of Mull. 23. Oransay, where St. Columba first landed on leaving Ireland. The island is separated from Colonsay only at floodtide. 24. Kilcholmkill, on the east coast of Islay. 25. Kilcholmkill, near Loch Finlagan, Islay. 26. Cove, on the west side of Loch Killisport. 27. Kilcolumkill, at the southern extremity of Cantyre. 28. St. Colomb's, a chapel in the parish of Rothesay, in Bute. 29. Kilmacolm (now Kilmal-colm), a parish in Renfrew. 30. Largs, in Ayrshire. The yearly fair held here in June is still called Colm's day. 31. Kirkcolm, a parish in Wigtown. 32. St. Columbo, a chapel at Caerlaverock, in Dumfries. The four last parishes were originally inhabited by *Australes Picti*, but in the time of Bede belonged to the *provincia Berniciorum*, and were thus under the rule of the Anglo-Saxon princes, who in the first half of the eighth century re-erected the see of St. Ninian, which in course of time had disappeared.

Among the Picts the following monasteries and churches were founded by or dedicated to St. Columba: 1. Burness, in Sanday, one of the Orkney Islands. 2. Hoy, one of the Orkneys. 3. St. Comb's, in Caithness. 4. Dirlet, in Caithness. 5. Island Comb, off the north coast of Sutherland, sometimes called the Island of Saints (*Eilean-na-naoimh*). 6. Killcolmkill, on Loch Brora, in Sutherland. 7. Auldearn, in Nairn, where St. Columba's Market is still held in June. 8. Pettie, in Invernessshire. 9. Kingussie, also in Invernessshire. The annual fair is held about St. Columba's day. 10. St. Colm's at Aird, in Banffshire. 11. Alvah, north-east of Banff. 12. Lonmay, in Aberdeenshire. 13. Daviot, 14. Belhelvie, and 15. Monycabo, all in Aberdeenshire. 16. Cortachy, in Forfarshire. 17. Tannadyce, south-east of the last. 18. Inchcolm, a small island in the Forth, where Alexander I erected a chapel in 1123 in fulfillment of a vow. He found a hermit upon the island, "dedicated to the service of St. Columba." 19. Dunkeld, in Perthshire—the most important foundation in connection with St. Columba's missionary labors among the southern Picts. On the death of King Brude, the faithful friend and supporter of the saint, he was succeeded by Gartnaidh, who belonged to the nation of the southern Picts, and who fixed his residence at Abernethy, on the bank of the Tay, near its junction with the Earn. It is told of him that he built the church of Abernethy two hundred and twenty-five years and eleven months before the foundation of the church of Dunkeld by King Constantine. Since the latter reigned from 790 to 820, and Gartnaidh from 584 to 599, the date of the foundation of Abernethy must have been between 584 and 596. The nation of the southern Picts had been converted by St. Ninian, and King Nectan (457–481) is said to have founded a church at Abernethy. These early labors had, however, no permanent results, and were followed, as we have seen, by a very general falling away from Christianity. King Gartnaidh built a new church, which was dedicated, as the first had been, to St. Bridget of Kildare. This foundation not only took place during St. Columba's life, but he was personally connected with it. In the tract known as the *Amra Columcille*, it is said, in allusion to his death, "For the teacher is not who used to teach the tribes of Toi"—that is, the tribes about the Tay—and again, "He subdued the mouths of the fierce who were at Toi with the will of the king," or as the gloss has it, "He subdued the mouths of the fierce with the *Ardig*, or supreme king of Toi." The king here referred to is Gartnaidh, and these words evidently point to the refounding of the church of Abernethy on the Tay, in connection with St. Columba's mission to the southern Picts. The saint was assisted in the work by St. Cainnach, who was himself of Pictish descent. Cainnach appears to have founded a monastery in the province of Fife, at the mouth of the river Eden, on the spot where afterward rose the celebrated church of St. Andrews. The churches dedicated to Saints Maluog, Drostan, Machut (a pupil of St. Brendan), and Cathan, and that founded at Dunblane by St. Blaan of Cinngaradh, son of King Aidan, give evidence of the spread of the Church among the southern Picts through the labors of St. Columba and his disciples.

In the latter years of his life, Columba revisited his beloved Ireland, and passed a few months in the celebrated monastery of Clonmacnois. The reception accorded to the venerable patriarch shows the high estimation in which he was held by the brethren. "As soon as it was known that he was near," says Adamnan, "all flocked from their little grange farms near the monastery, and, along with those who were within it, ranged themselves with enthusiasm under the Abbot Alither; then advancing beyond the enclosure of the monastery, they went out as one man to meet St. Columba, as if he were an angel of the Lord. Humbly bowing down, with their faces to the ground, in his presence, they kissed him most reverently, and singing hymns of praise as they went, they conducted him with all honor to the church. Over the saint, as he walked, a canopy made of wood was supported by four men walking by his side, lest the holy Abbot St. Columba should be troubled by the crowd of brethren pressing upon him." In the year 593 the saint completed the thirtieth year of his missionary life in Scotland. He seems already to have had a presentiment of his approaching death, which did not, however, take place until 597. It was in the last few years of his life that he is said, according to a venerable tradition, to have visited the tombs of the Apostles. This tradition is referred to in the ancient Irish Life of the saint, as well as in the biography of St. Mochonna. It was also preserved, as Cardinal Moran relates, by the old Guides of the Vatican, who pointed out in the ancient Basilica of St. Peter's the exact spot on which St. Gregory the Great had given the kiss of peace to the renowned apostle of the Picts. Not long after the latter's return to Iona, seven monks arrived thither from Rome, bringing to him on behalf of the Pontiff a collection of Latin hymns, besides other costly gifts. Among the latter was the so-called "great gem of Columcille," shaped in the form of a cross. This was for centuries an object of religious veneration to the community of Iona, and afterward belonged to the monastery of Tory Island, off the coast of Donegal, where it was still preserved in the sixteenth century. St. Columba in return bestowed rich gifts on the Roman messengers, and in particular desired them to present to Pope Gregory the hymn *"Altus prosator,"* which he had composed a short time before, and which the Pontiff is said in the ancient record to have highly commended and esteemed. Adamnan might thus well write of St. Columba, that "his name has not only become illustrious throughout Ireland and Britain, but has reached even unto triangular Spain, and into Gaul, and to Italy, which lies beyond the Pennine Alps; and also to the city of Rome itself, the head of all cities."

Last days

The narrative given us of the last days of Columba's earthly pilgrimage is singularly touching. Toward the end of May 597, the holy abbot desired to visit the western part of Iona. Unable, through age and weakness, to proceed thither on foot, he was carried in a car drawn by oxen. When the brethren had gathered round him, he said: "During the Paschal solemnities in the month of April now past, with desire have I desired to depart to Christ the Lord, as He had allowed me, if I preferred it. But lest a joyous festival should be turned for you into mourning, I thought it better to put off for a little longer the time of my departure from the world." At these words the brethren broke out into tears and lamentations, while Columba, still seated in his chariot, blessed the island with its inhabitants, and was carried back to his monastery. On the following Saturday, the saint, leaning on his faithful attendant Diarmaid, went to bless the granary. "This day," said Columba, "in the Holy Scriptures is called the Sabbath, which means rest. And this day is indeed a Sabbath to me, for it is the last day of my present laborious life, and on it I rest after the fatigues of my labors; and this night at midnight, which commences the solemn Lord's Day, I shall go the way of our fathers. For already my Lord Jesus Christ deigns to invite me; and to Him, I say, in the middle of this night shall I depart at His invitation." As the saint returned homeward, he rested at a spot afterward marked by a cross, and where still stands one of the ancient Celtic crosses of Iona. While he sat there, the old white horse of the monastery came up to him and, laying its head in his bosom, began to lament his approaching death with plaintive cries. Columba would not allow Diarmaid to drive it away. Presently, ascending the hill which overlooked the monastery, with hands uplifted to heaven he blessed the monastery in these words: "Small and mean though this place is, yet it shall be held in great and unusual honor, not only by the Irish kings and people, but also by foreign chiefs and barbarous nations; even the saints of other Churches shall regard it with no common reverence."

Then returning to his cell, he began to work at a transcription of the Psalter, in which he had for a long time been occupied. When he had written these words of the thirty-third Psalm, "They who seek the Lord shall want nothing that is good," he paused, and said, "Here must I end; let Baithene write what follows." For the last time he assembled the brethren round his dying bed. "These, my children," he said, "are the last words I address to you—that you be at peace and have unfeigned charity among yourselves; and if you thus follow the example of the holy fathers, God, the comforter of the good, will be your helper, and I, abiding with Him, will intercede for you; and He will not only give you sufficient to supply the wants of this present life, but will also bestow on you the good and eternal rewards of those who keep His commandments." With these words the venerable patriarch became silent, and the brethren departed. At midnight, however, at the first sound of the bell which called the community to prayer, he hastened to the church before all the rest, knelt down at the foot of the altar, and blessing for the last time the assembled brethren, breathed forth his pure soul in Diarmaid's arms, on the morning of Sunday the 9th of June 597, after an apostolate of thirty-four years among the Pictish people.

The Comte de Montalembert, in his brilliant picture of Western monachism, *The Monks of the West from St. Benedict to St. Bernard*, has portrayed in vivid colors the character and labors of St. Columba. It seems to us, however, that the celebrated historian has not done full justice to the character of the saint. His biographer, Adamnan, whose work bears all the marks of care, and who in its compilation had undoubtedly much written material at his disposal, has presented to us a picture of his hero, from which the almost irreconcilable contrasts found by Montalembert in Columba's character are wholly absent. The estimate of Montalembert is in truth based, as Dr. Skene has well pointed out, on facts which will not stand the test of critical examination, and he has portrayed features in the saint's character which we seek in vain in the early and authentic Lives. Before taking leave of the patriarch of Scottish monks, let us see what is the testimony given of him by men separated from his own days by a space of time comparatively short.

"From his boyhood," writes Adamnan, Columba's successor in the government of the monastery of Iona, "he had been brought up in Christian training in the study of wisdom, and by the grace of God had so preserved the integrity of his body and the purity of his soul that, though dwelling on earth, he appeared to live like the saints in heaven. For he was angelic in appearance, graceful in speech, holy in work, with talents of the highest order, and consummate prudence. He lived a soldier of Christ during thirty-four years on an island. He never could spend the space even of one hour without study, or prayer, or writing, or some other holy occupation. So incessantly was he engaged night and day in the unwearied exercise of fasting and watching, that the burden of each of these austerities would seem beyond the power of all human endurance. And still, in all these, he was beloved by all; for a holy joy ever beaming on his face revealed the joy and gladness with which the Holy Spirit filled his inmost soul."

In complete harmony with this picture of St. Columba is that given us by Dalian Forgaill in the ancient tract called the *Amra Columcille* which we have already cited. The people, he tells us, mourned for him who was "their souls' light, their learned one—their chief from right—who was God's messenger—who dispelled fears from them—who used to explain the truth of words; a harp without a base chord—a perfect sage who believed Christ. He was learned, he was chaste, he was charitable—an abounding benefit unto guests; he was eager, he was noble, he was gentle; he was the physician of the heart to every sage—he was to persons inscrutable—he was a shelter to the naked—he was a consolation to the poor." We see indeed, in St. Columba, a force of character well-nigh irresistible—we recognize in him a man born to leave upon his age and country the impress of his lofty soul in indelible characters. It was the spirit of Christianity which permeated his whole being, and to which the service of his life was devoted—that softened down every harshness, every asperity of his natural disposition, so that his pure and childlike soul attached to itself almost involuntarily every heart that came within its influence.

CHAPTER 3

THE CLOISTER LIFE OF IONA

The rule of the community

The question has been often asked whether the Rule of Columba or any of his contemporaries promulgated a new monastic rule. Reyner was of the contrary opinion; and although Fleming and O'Conor disagreed with him on the point, they have been unable to support their own view by any positive proofs. St. Wilfrid indeed, in his speech at the synod of Whitby, on the subject of the Paschal reckoning, spoke of the *regula ac praecepta* of St. Columba; but neither here, nor in the ancient Lives of the Irish saints, are we to understand the word *regula* in the sense of written rules, but far more frequently with the signification of "discipline" or "observance." It was no doubt the general belief in the Middle Ages that the fathers of the Irish Church had designed and established various religious orders differing from each other in rule and practice. An ancient Life of St. Kieran of Clonmacnois mentions eight of these, attributing them respectively to Patrick, Brandan, Kieran, Columba, Comgall, Adamnan, Bridget, and Lisrian. There are grave reasons, however, against the authenticity of this enumeration. As far as Adamnan is concerned, instead of being the introducer of a new rule into his community, he was not even able to induce them to accept the reformed Paschal canon. The Burgundian Library in Brussels contains an MS. copy of the so-called Rule of St. Columba. A single glance at its contents, however, is sufficient to show that this lucubration is merely an instruction for the eremitical life, and by no means puts before us such a body of rules as would be required for the manifold life and labors of the community of Iona. It is remarkable, moreover, that the learned Franciscan Colgan, who lived before the dispersion of the Irish records and had the best opportunity for discovering the ancient monastic rules, should have known nothing of this pretended Rule of St. Columba. The only authentic documents of the sort which have come down to us are the Rule of St. Columbanus and the Penitentials of Columbanus and Cummian. Lucas Holstenius has, it is true, published two Rules—one entitled *Cujusdam Patris Regula ad Monachos*, consisting of thirty-two chapters, and the other *Cujusdam Patris Regula ad Virgines*, of twenty-four chapters—which are attributed by Calmet to St. Comgall, but by Holstenius himself to St. Columba. These are, however, pure conjectures, unsupported in the slightest degree either by external evidence or by the contents of the Rules in question. Nor can the *Ordo Monasticus*, printed by Holstenius and ascribed by him to "ancient Scottish monks," put forward any better claim to authenticity. Holstenius lived at a time when questions regarding the introduction of Christianity into Scotland and its first apostle were still enveloped in obscurity, which has been only partially dispelled by the researches of modem students.

We are nevertheless by no means without information regarding the life and discipline of the monks of Iona. Scattered through Adamnan's Life are numerous notices, which, when carefully brought together, furnish an almost complete picture of the cloister life; and some particulars of information are likewise afforded by the writings of Bede.

The life of the community of Iona, like that of all religious orders of the Catholic Church, had for its foundation the idea of the *militia Christi*—the warfare of Christ—and he who adopted it became thereby a soldier of the Lord, and the *commilito* of his religious brethren. The novice at his entrance professed his readiness to renounce the cares of the world, to offer himself to God's service, and to become an *athleta Christi*, for the one end and object of the spread of the Gospel. The community bore the name of a college of monks and consisted of a family or spiritual organization, with the abbot at its head.

The abbot, called "father," "holy father," or "holy elder," and, when also the founder, "patron," had his seat at the mother church—that is, at Iona, which was distinguished by the title of *insula primaria*. His jurisdiction was not limited to his own monastery, but extended equally over all the affiliated churches in Scotland as well as Ireland, which he visited canonically at fixed times, and whose superiors were appointed by him and were bound to receive and to carry out his orders. Being only a priest in ecclesiastical rank, he was styled emphatically *abbas et presbyter*, and could perform, of course, only priestly functions. This, however, was merely a local observance, the highest development of the second order of saints, in which, as we have already seen, the priestly order preponderated: it by no means implied any disregard of the episcopal office. In the monastery of Iona, as well as in other communities, there were always certain monks who had received episcopal consecration, and were accordingly competent to exercise the corresponding functions. The exercise of their episcopal authority, however, remained subject to the jurisdiction of the abbot, on whose responsibility their acts were usually performed. Ranking above the abbot in ecclesiastical position, they were nevertheless subordinate to him in all that regarded the government of the community. Columba himself, as Adamnan tells us, was scrupulous in his recognition of the episcopal precedence, and gave place unhesitatingly to the bishop at the altar. Opportunities of showing such deference were not lacking, for Irish bishops were very frequent visitors to his monastery. The abbot was wont to assemble the brethren in the oratory, where he instructed them in the spiritual life: these conferences were sometimes held at midnight. From him emanated the regulation of the order of the day, as well as of the celebration of festivals, dispensing of fasts, or improvements in discipline. His blessing was asked and obtained before leaving the monastery on a journey. The brethren saluted him by prostrating on the ground. To the abbot, moreover, belonged the administration of the temporalities. When at home he was always attended by one or other of the community; and on a journey he was accompanied by a party, termed *viri sociales*. The administration of baptism and preaching were functions usually performed by him in preference to other members of the community. As already mentioned, it was Columba who officiated at the solemn coronation of King Aidan of Dalriada in Iona; and the function most probably continued to be the exclusive privilege of his successors. The founder of the monastery named his own successor, one who had been his *alumnus*. The subsequent abbots were elected in conformity with the Irish usage, which gave to founders' kin preference over all other candidates. Of the eleven immediate successors of Columba, Suibhne is the only one of uncertain pedigree, and there is but one (Connamail, the tenth abbot) descended from a different house. The same custom was rigidly adhered to until the year 716, when the ancient observance of Easter and the Celtic tonsure were abandoned. The result of this was a break in the old monastic tradition, and the consequent introduction of the free right of election to the abbacy.

The community was termed *muintir*, in Latin *familia*, and consisted of brothers, called by the abbot *fratres*, or sometimes *filii*. Their numbers, at first limited to twelve, were afterward largely increased, and included both Britons and Saxons. The brethren of proved stability were known as seniors; those still under instruction as juniors or *alumni*; while those who possessed special aptitude for manual labor were called operarii fratres, or working brothers. Besides the community, properly so called, there were generally in the monastery a certain number of penitents, sometimes called *proselyti*, and of guests.

Thus constituted, the monastic family was regulated by the two great principles of obedience and brotherly love. The precept of St. Columbanus—"At the first word of the senior it behooves all to rise and obey, because their obedience is thus paid to God, according to the saying of our Lord Jesus Christ, 'He who hears you, hears me'"—was observed not less strictly in Iona. Hence the readiness of the brethren to prepare, at the shortest notice, for long and difficult journeys, to take on themselves the service of the monastery, to work in the open air in the most inclement weather, to sacrifice cherished customs; hence, too, the severe rebuke which followed any infringement of obedience.

Private property was unknown; everything was held in common. "Be always naked"—so ran Columba's eremitical rule—"in imitation of Christ, and according to the precepts of the Gospel." In harmony with this is the injunction of St. Columbanus, "Nakedness and contempt of wealth are the first perfection of monks."

The narrative of Adamnan leaves no room for doubt that St. Columba held Christian matrimony in honor, and was ever ready and desirous to promote conjugal happiness. For himself, however, and his disciples, in conformity with the lofty ideal at which they aimed—nothing less, indeed, than the closest union with God—the principle he inculcated was that of St. Columbanus: "*Virgo corpore et virgo mente.*" Celibacy was therefore the constant rule in Iona, and anything like a hereditary succession in the abbacy was consequently excluded. If, among the secular clergy, we find instances here and there of so-called marriage ties, they are not to be regarded as evidence of a permanent and recognized institution; on the contrary, such unions were, even then, considered unlawful both in Scotland and in Ireland, and were repudiated not only by regulars, but by the law of the universal Church. There is nothing in the narrative of Adamnan which affords the slightest support to the theory of a married clergy; it merely records an abuse which met with the summary vengeance of heaven.

Fraternal love and humility were the principles which governed the monks in their intercourse with one another. Whoever, for any transgression, received a rebuke from the abbot, had, in sign of penance, to prostrate on the ground until the blessing of his superior permitted him to rise. Hospitality, a striking feature in all ancient monasteries, was preeminently so in Iona, fostered as it was by the natural kindliness and generosity of the Celtic character; and Adamnan relates numerous anecdotes which have reference to it. The guest, after receiving from the abbot the kiss of peace, was conducted to the *hospitium*, where his needs were supplied; and the community were so far affected by his presence that the abbot, should it happen to be a fast-day, gave permission, in honor of the guest, for *consolatio cibi*. Abundant alms were dispensed by the abbot, where necessity claimed relief. In the same way as, up to the present day, the monasteries of Italy possessed admirable dispensaries, so the monks of St. Columba were accustomed to furnish medical advice and assistance to the sick and suffering.

Services and sacraments

A prominent feature of the cloister life of Iona was the solemn performance of divine service. The days were divided into working and holy days. On the former, the offices of the Church were carried out by the monastic community, strictly so called, while the lay brethren were employed in field work. On Sundays and holy days all the inmates of the monastery were bound to be present. These days were distinguished by a solemn celebration of the holy mysteries, abstinence from manual work, and some addition to the ordinary fare. The office began on the eve of the feast, in the regular manner, by the celebration of vespers, called by Adamnan *missa vespertinalis*, or sometimes simply *missa*. The central act of worship consisted in the holy sacrifice of the Mass. The expressions employed by Adamnan afford indisputable proof of the union of the Scottish and Irish Churches at this time with the Catholic Church in every part of the Christian world. Were there more than one priest present, the consecration was performed by all in common, in token of their equal dignity. Should a bishop, however, be among them, the privilege of offering the holy sacrifice was reserved exclusively to him, in deference to his more exalted rank. The brethren approached the altar, and received the Holy Eucharist from the hands of the celebrant.

The principal festival was Easter, on which observance the whole community received Holy Communion. Easter time was a season of joy; and the seven weeks between Easter and Pentecost were known as the Easter Days. With regard to the time for observing Easter, the monks of Iona clung tenaciously to their ancient mode of reckoning, differing thereby sometimes almost a month from the observance of the rest of Christendom. It was not until 716 that they submitted to the introduction of the calendar as amended by the Holy See. Next in order to Easter ranked the feast of Christmas, which was preceded by a fast of forty days. We are told of St. Columba that he showed special zeal in the observance of fasting. Excepting between Easter and Pentecost, every Wednesday and Friday was a fast-day. Neither food nor drink was taken until after noon, provided that consideration for guests did not demand an exception to the rule.

During the forty days of Lent, the fast was not permitted to be broken until the evening.

In addition to the Eucharistic worship, the other sacraments were also duly administered. The baptism of adult converts was preceded by proper instruction in faith and morals. Holy orders were conferred only by a bishop; but before the ordination of a priest, the abbot also laid his right hand on the head of the candidate, thereby signifying his concurrence in the act of ordination. The consecration of the Bishops Aidan, Finan, Colman, and Cellach in Iona proves the presence of at least one bishop in the monastery. If the consecration was canonically performed, three bishops must have assisted at it—not, however, all belonging to the monastery, but brought for the occasion from other Irish or Scottish houses. We know that St. Finan consecrated Cedd with the assistance of two other bishops. Cases, however, occur in which a single prelate officiated. St. Kentigern, for example, received consecration from one bishop only. Archbishops Lanfranc and St. Anselm of Canterbury censured the practice as existing in Ireland in their time.

The ancient Scottish monasteries were places not only of prayer but also of Christian penance. A number of persons—not, strictly speaking, members of the community—were nevertheless received and permitted to wear the clerical habit. These were penitents desirous of expiating their sins. The work of penance was perfected by slow degrees. The brother who had been guilty of a transgression was required to acknowledge it in presence of the entire community, usually on his knees. On promising amendment, absolution was granted him by the abbot, who at the same time prescribed a suitable penance. This often consisted in banishment to some subordinate house, where the delinquent might remain as much as ten years in the practice of works of mortification and penance. The most severe punishment was perpetual banishment from the country.

Customs

The monks of Iona wore the so-called tonsure of Simon Magus, in which the anterior part only of the head was shaved—i.e., from ear to ear—as opposed to the Greek tonsure, in which the whole head, and to the Roman, in which merely the crown, was made bare. The introduction of the reformed Easter reckoning in 716 was followed two years later by the adoption of the Roman tonsure. The advocates of this alleged the supposed connection of the Celtic form of tonsure with Simon Magus as a reason for its abolition; and we find from Adamnan's reply to Ceolfrid, when the latter reproached him with wearing the "tonsure of Simon," that he seems to have tacitly acquiesced in the charge.

The burial of the dead was an important feature of the monastic life of Iona. The lively faith in the resurrection of the body, which illuminated the earthly pilgrimage of the monk, led him to attribute great importance to honorable sepulture. It was in the midst of his brethren that he desired to await the final awakening from his long sleep. The lifeless remains were wrapped in white linen and laid out first in the cell, afterward in the church, where were performed the funeral rites, consisting of prayers, chants, and the oblation of the holy sacrifice. The body was then borne in solemn procession to its last resting place.

The manifold use of the sign of the holy cross has yet to be mentioned. To the monk of Iona, as to Christians of every age, it was the *signum salutare*, the sign of salvation. Before he went forth to the work of his daily life, or made use of any tool, he made the sacred sign. By it demons were put to flight, wild beasts were overcome, locked doors were burst open, and bodily infirmities healed. The numerous incidents of the kind, narrated by Adamnan in his Life of St. Columba, carry us back involuntarily to the three first Christian centuries, when the sign of the cross exercised so potent an influence over external nature and on the bodies of men. Hence, doubtless, sprang that deep reverence for the cross among the monks of Iona, which led them to mark every remarkable event connected with the history of their institute by the erection of a cross. At one time the island possessed not less than three hundred and sixty such crosses. Even the masts and yards of their ships were arranged in cruciform fashion. Food and drink, and the very tools used for the daily labor, were blessed with the holy sign, and thus set apart to the service of God.

Besides prayer and manual labor, the monks had also to devote themselves at due times to reading and writing. The principal study was that of the Holy Scriptures, and, in particular, the Psalms of David, which had to be learned by heart. Profane learning, however, was by no means neglected: on the contrary, the Greek and Latin languages were zealously cultivated. The Latin writings of Adamnan, as well as Cummian's Epistle on Easter, afford ample testimony of their classical attainments. For public reading, they had, besides Adamnan's Life of their founder, the biography of St. Martin of Sulpicius Severus, and that of St. Germanus by Constantine. Every monastery possessed its Scriptorium, where the manuscripts were written. These were chiefly liturgical books, for use in the divine office in the different churches of the Order. Numerous copies, too, were transcribed of the Sacred Scriptures. The manuscripts were usually devoid of ornament; but the Books of Kells and Durrow, which, with their sumptuous illuminations, are still preserved, bear striking witness to the artistic skill of the Columban monks. St. Columba's immediate successor, St. Baithene, who was a calligrapher of renown, executed with great accuracy a large number of transcriptions of the Gospel. In many cases the practice was adopted of writing Latin in Greek letters, as is exemplified in parts of the Book of Armagh. There is little doubt that in Iona, as in other medieval monasteries, a book of annals was kept, in which were chronicled memorable events relating to the institution.

The habit of the monks consisted of the cowl, or upper garment, and the tunic, worn underneath it. Both were made of wool and of a white color. In severe weather a warmer cloak, called the *amphibalus*, was worn over the tunic. During labor the brothers wore sandals, which were laid aside at meals. The cells were provided with beds (*lectuli*), finished each with a straw mattress and pillow.

In taking leave of the great foundation of St. Columba, it will not be out of place to record some of those principles of the monastic life, as found in his Rule, which he was wont to inculcate on his disciples. "A mind prepared for red martyrdom. A mind fortified and steadfast for white martyrdom. Forgiveness from the heart to everyone. Constant prayers for those who trouble you. Follow alms-giving before all things. Take not of food till you are hungry. The love of God with all your heart and all your strength. The love of your neighbor as yourself. Abide in God's testaments throughout all times. Thy measure of prayer shall be until your tears come; or your measure of work of labor until your tears come."

The regulations of the cloister life of Iona, especially the importance attached to the Episcopate, and to holy Mass and the divine office, leave no room for doubt that St. Columba and his spiritual children formed no isolated fragment of Christendom, but were united in life and in with the universal Catholic Church. The theory upheld down to our own days by Presbyterian historians, that the Reformation was built up on the primitive lines, and was in fact a revival of Christianity uncorrupted by human frailty, was founded on a defective knowledge of the Columban Church. Subsequent researches have made it abundantly clear that the ancient Celtic Church, apart from some few differences in ceremonial matters, differed in no single point of importance from the universal Church.

ST. COLUMBA'S SUCCESSORS
IN IONA

The connection of Iona with Northumbria

In continuation of our sketch of the history of the monastery of Iona, we shall proceed to trace its development until the beginning of the eighth century, dwelling upon its relations with the church of Northumbria, and proceeding thereafter to treat of the missionary labors of St. Kentigern among the Britons of Strathclyde.

The monastery of Iona, in which the great patriarch of the Scottish monks labored and ended his days, was considered the mother house of the monasteries founded by Columba in Scotland and Ireland, and all the rest owed it obedience. "This monastery," observes Bede, "for a long time held the preeminence over most of those of the northern Scots, and all those of the Picts, and had the direction of their people," and he gives as a reason for this distinction the fact that Iona possessed the body of the founder. Columba's successors in office maintained this preeminence. "For," says Bede, "whatever kind of person he was himself, this we know of him for certain, that he left successors distinguished for their great charity, divine love, and strict attention to the rules of discipline; following, indeed, uncertain cycles in their computation of the great festival [of Easter] because, far away as they were out of the world, no one had supplied them with the synodal decrees relating to the Paschal observance; yet withal diligently observing such works of piety and charity as they could find in the prophetic, evangelical, and apostolic writings."

On Columba's decease, his cousin Baithene, according to the law which prevailed in the Irish monasteries, was appointed Abbot of Iona. He was superior of the monastery of Maigh Lunge in Tiree, and descended from the northern Hy-Neills; and he had doubtless been designated by St. Columba himself as his successor. "It was from the men of Erin," says the Martyrology of Donegal, "that the abbot of Hy was chosen, and he was most frequently chosen from the men of Cinel Conaill." Baithene held his high office only for two years. He died in 599, on the same day of the year as St. Columba.

His successor was Laisren, who had been Abbot of Durrow, in Ireland, during St. Columba's life. It was during his term of office that the celebrated discussions relative to the keeping of Easter began in Britain. The mission to Gaul in 590 of Columbanus, who vehemently defended his national customs, and the dispatch of Augustine to Britain by St. Gregory, were the immediate occasion of those frequently renewed disputes which lasted for more than a century, and only ended with the adoption of the Roman reckoning by the monks of Iona, in 716. Laurence, who succeeded St. Augustine in 604, "not only," says Bede, "attended to the charge of the new Church that was gathered from the English people, but also regarded with pastoral solicitude the old natives of Britain, and likewise the people of the Scots who inhabit the island of Ireland adjacent to Britain. In conjunction with his fellow bishops he addressed the following letter to the Irish hierarchy: "To our lords and most dear brethren the bishops or abbots throughout all Scotia, Laurentius, Mellitus, and Justus, bishops, the servants of the servants of God. When the Apostolic See, according to her practice in all the world, stationed us in these Western parts to preach to the pagan nations here, and so it came to pass that we entered into this island which is called Britain, before we were acquainted with it, supposing that they walked in the ways of the universal Church, we felt a very high respect for the Britons as well as the Scots, from our regard for their sanctity of character; but when we came to know the Britons, we supposed the Scots must be superior to them. However, we have learned from Bishop Daganus coming into this island, and Abbot Columbanus coming into Gaul, that the Scots differ not at all from the Britons in their habits. For Bishop Daganus, when he came to us, would not take meat with us, no, not so much as in the same lodging where we were eating." This letter shows something of the spirit which prevailed; but it was followed by no result. Each side clung tenaciously to its own customs.

Abbot Laisren died in 605 and was succeeded Fergna, surnamed Brit, or the Briton, albeit he too was of St. Columba's family and descended from Conall Gulban. He had been educated in Iona, under the saintly founder. Adamnan, who calls him Virgnous (the Latin form of Fergna) speaks of him as "a youth of good disposition, and afterward made by God superior of this church, in which I, though unworthy, now serve." His period of rule was marked by several important events. Tighernach records in the year 617 the martyrdom of Domian of Egg, with his fifty-two companions. He is thus commemorated, on May 17, in the Calendar of Marianus Gorman: "Donnan the Great with his monks: fifty-two were his congregation. There came pirates of the sea to the island in which they were, and slew them all. Eig is the name of that island." Egg is the most easterly of a group of islands lying between Ardnamurchan Point and the Isle of Skye. It was at this time under the rule of a pagan queen, to whom the young Christian colony of Egg was doubtless obnoxious, and who therefore employed pirates to set fire to their wooden church, and to murder the monks while engaged in the holy sacrifice. Angus the Culdee tells the tale of their martyrdom. The queen was told that Donnan and his companions had taken up their abode in a place where her sheep were kept. "'Let them all be killed,' said she. 'That would not be a religious act,' said her people. But they were murderously assailed. At this time the clerics were at mass. 'Let us have respite till mass is ended,' said Donnan. 'You shall have it,' said they. And when it was over, they were slain every one of them." The Irish Annals record in the year 616 the death of Tolorggain, or Talarican, whom the Scottish Calendars associate with the church of Fordyce, on the southern shore of the Moray Firth.

The most important event, however, of this period was the arrival of certain noble Angles at Iona in the year 617; for it was the occasion of the extension of the Columban Church to the kingdom of Northumbria. Ethelfrid, the pagan king of Bernicia, who had defeated the Scottish king Aidan in the great battle of Dawston in 606, was in his turn defeated in 617 by Edwin, King of Deira, and Bernicia and Deira were united into one kingdom. Ethelfrid's sons, Ainfrid, Osay, and Oswald, together with the flower of the nobility, fled before the conqueror, and took refuge among the Picts or Scots, where they lived in exile during the reign of Edwin, and, Bede tells us, "were there catechized according to the doctrine of the Scots, and regenerated by the grace of baptism." Prominent among them was Oswald, the second son of Ethelfrid. There is no doubt that by the "refuge among the Scots" Bede alludes to Iona. Oswald remained there until 633, including therefore the whole term of office of Fergna, who died in 623, and ten years of his successors.

Seguine, son of Fiachna and nephew of Laisren, the third abbot, held office from 623 to 652. Under him the Columban Church became highly flourishing. King Edwin, after his conquest of Ethelfrid, had been converted to Christianity, conversion His wife, the daughter of the Christian king of Edwin and Kent, had been accompanied to York by Paulinus, recently consecrated bishop by Archbishop Justus of Canterbury. Paulinus baptized Edwin on Easter Sunday 627 at York, in the wooden church which he had built when a catechumen. Here Edwin erected an episcopal see for his instructor, Paulinus. The inhabitants of Deira and Bernicia, now united under one scepter, followed the example of their monarch. Pope Honorius I (625–638) received with joy the tidings of the conversion of the kingdom of Northumbria, wrote to the king a letter of congratulation, exhorting him and his people to perseverance, and sent the pallium to Paulinus. But when the apostolic brief reached York, Edwin had been totally defeated and slain by the united armies of the pagan princes Penda of Mercia and Cadwalla of Wales at the battle of Hathfield in 633. Paulinus was forced to fly, and Christianity in Northumbria was trodden down under the iron heel of the conqueror. A brighter future, however, was about to dawn on the land. Oswald, who, in consequence of the assassination of his elder brother Ainfrid by Cadwalla, now claimed the Northumbrian throne, collected a force and recovered his kingdom by a victory over Cadwalla at the battle of Hefenveld, near Hexham, in 634. The first object of the pious monarch was the restoration of the Christian religion in Northumbria. With this aim it was natural that he should place himself in communication with the Scots, from whom he had himself received the light of faith. From them he asked for a bishop, and received one in the person of Aidan—"a man," says Bede, "of singular meekness, piety, and moderation." We are told that the Scots first sent to Oswald a missionary of more austere character, who, however, far from meeting with success in his labors, incurred the dislike of the Angles and was forced to return home. A great council was then held, in which Aidan rose and addressed him thus:

"I am of opinion, brother, that you were more severe to your unlearned hearers than you ought to have been, and did not at first, conformably to the apostolic discipline, give them the milk of more gentle doctrine, till, being by degrees nourished with the Word of God, they should be capable of greater perfection, and able to practice God's sublimer precepts." At these prudent words all eyes were turned on the orator, who seemed to them to be himself the most fitted to succeed in the difficult task. Aidan was, according to Bede, a monk of Iona, "whose monastery," he adds, "for a long time held the preeminence over almost all those of the northern Scots and all those of the Picts." The Abbot of Iona at this time was, as we have said, Segine, under whom was held the council relating to the missionary revival in Northumbria. He had probably, on the failure of the first missionaries, gone thither personally in order to inform himself as to the country; for Adamnan mentions a conversation which took place, according to him, between King Oswald and Abbot Segine after the battle of Hefenveld.

The holy island of Lindisfarne

The first Scottish apostles to Northumbria had been simple priests; the head of the new mission was to receive episcopal orders. Whether one bishop or three officiated at his consecration cannot now be ascertained; but, as we know, bishops were not wanting in the Columban monasteries. We are expressly told that the abbots of Lismore and Kingarth held episcopal rank, besides which the cooperation of bishops from Ireland could be obtained for the consecration. The distance of Northumbria from Scotland, as well as the due advancement of the Church in that remote country, would render it necessary for the head of the new mission to receive episcopal orders. In other respects, however, the monastic character of the Scottish Church was prominent in its Northumbrian offshoot. The new bishop did not establish himself at York, where Edwin had fixed the episcopal see, but in the island of Lindisfarne, on the coast of Northumbria, which thus became, as Bede observes, at the same time the seat of a bishop and the residence of an abbot and his monks. "Yea," he adds, "all whom it contains are monks; for Aidan, who was the first bishop of the place, was a monk, and was always wont to lead a monastic life, with all his people. Hence, after him, all the bishops of that place until this day exercise the episcopal functions in such sort, that, while the abbot, who is chosen by the bishop with the consent of the brethren, governs the monastery, all the priests, deacons, chanters, readers, and other ecclesiastical orders, with the bishop himself, observe in all things the monastic rule." Bede proceeds to draw a glowing picture of the zeal with which the Scottish missionaries who came daily into Britain preached the Word of God and, if in priestly orders, administered the Sacraments. He speaks further of churches being built and lauds especially the generosity of King Oswald in granting lands for this purpose.

The episcopate of Aidan in Northumbria forms one of the most beautiful chapters in English and Scottish ecclesiastical history; and on account of the close relations which he ever maintained with his northern home, it must be briefly touched upon. "No sacred spot in Britain," says Bright, "is worthier of a reverential visit than this Holy Island of Aidan and his successors"—an opinion expressed in pregnant words by the learned Alcuin a thousand years before. Lying off the Northumberland coast, between the frontier town of Berwick and the ancient feudal fortress of Bamborough, and connected with the mainland only at low water, Lindisfarne, both in its exterior formation and its climatic conditions, resembles in a remarkable degree the mother island of Iona. Both islands, once the seats of holy monks and bishops, the work of whose lives was labor, prayer, and learning, the spread of the Gospel, and the civilization of nations, now bear alike the stamp of desolation and melancholy. From Lindisfarne Aidan ruled his widely scattered diocese, which extended from the Humber to the Firth of Forth. He was inspired, Bede tells us, with a passionate love of virtue, but at the same time full of a surpassing mildness and gentleness. His generosity in alms-giving was boundless. His only drink was water or milk, and his monks shared his abstemiousness. It was not until a hundred years later, when Ceolwulf, King of Northumbria, came to Lind-isfarne and laid down his crown at the tomb of the saint, that permission was given to taste wine or beer. Aidan established the custom of fasting until three o'clock on Wednesday and Friday. One of his favorite occupations was the study of Holy Scripture. He founded numerous churches, to serve which he brought over priests from Ireland; but he fostered vocations also among the youth of the country, and twelve young men of noble birth were instructed and educated for the priesthood under his direction at Lindisfarne. As he was at first unacquainted with the Anglo-Saxon tongue, King Oswald accompanied him on his missionary journeys and acted as his interpreter. Oswald's younger brother and successor, Oswy, King of Bernicia, was no less well disposed. Little wonder, then, that Aidan's glowing zeal should have won the victory for Christianity in Northumbria. Bede lays special stress on the fact that the holy bishop gained the love and veneration even of those who differed from him as to the celebration of Easter. "His keeping the Pasch out of its time," writes Bede, "I do not approve nor commend; but this I do approve of, that what he kept in thought, reverenced, and preached in the celebration of his paschal festival, was just what we ourselves do—that is, the redemption of mankind through the passion, resurrection, and ascension into heaven of Jesus Christ, the mediator between God and man."

Among Aidan's chief foundations were the two great mon-asteries of Melrose and Coldingham. The former of these (sometimes called Old Melrose, to distinguish it from the later Cistercian abbey of the same name) was situated about two miles west of the present town of Melrose, not far from the point where the river Leader flows into the Tweed. Its first abbot was Eata, one of Aidan's most beloved disciples. For two hundred years this monastery was a center of Christian life and learning, until destroyed by an invasion of the Scots in the year 839. Coldingham, the second famous foundation of Aidan, called by Bede *Urbs Coludi*, was built upon a rock overhanging the sea. It was a so-called double monastery, containing two distinct communities of men and women. It was long governed by St. Ebba, the first abbess, to whom the Irish monk Adamnan foretold that the monastery would after her death be destroyed by fire. The prophecy was duly fulfilled; and Bede adds, "as all who knew the case could well perceive, by a heavy vengeance from heaven." On the 31st of August, 651, after a life full of labor and merit, the holy Bishop Aidan breathed his last in a little church near the royal residence at Bamborough. The spot on which he died, and where stands a chapel bearing his name, is still pointed out. His mortal remains were taken to Lindisfarne and temporarily deposited there until they found a permanent resting place beside the altar of the noble church erected on the island a little later.

The date of Easter

The year 634, in which the Columban Church was transplanted by St. Aidan to Northumbria, is memorable also for the adoption of the Roman tonsure and Easter reckoning by the southern Picts in Ireland. Segine, Abbot of Iona, received news of this in a letter from Cummian, one of the most learned ecclesiastics of the time, who appears to have been abbot of the great monastery of Durrow, founded by St. Columba. In this important document, of which we give a summary, Cummian begins by speaking of the aversion which he had felt toward the Roman rite on its first appearance in Ireland. For a whole year he had retired into the sanctuary of God—that is, the Holy Scriptures—and given to the subject his most anxious consideration. He had also devoted much study to historical works, and such cycles as he was able to meet with. This investigation, he added, had induced him to adopt the Roman mode of reckoning. When a year had elapsed, he had applied to the successors of the fathers of his Church, of Ailbe, Kieran, and Brendan, and asked their opinion of the excommunication which had been pronounced against them by the Holy See. These having assembled in council on the plain of Lene, where the monastery of Durrow was situated, announced as the result of their deliberations that they ought to adopt the practice followed by the successors of the Apostles; and he was consequently enjoined to act accordingly. Fresh opposition, however, having sprung up, certain "wise and humble" men had been deputed to proceed to Rome, where they lived for three years in one house with a Greek, a Hebrew, a Scythian, and an Egyptian. All these celebrated Easter together in St. Peter's Church, the Scots alone differing by a whole month from the observance of the Apostolic See. A number of testimonies from the Fathers followed relative to the duty of subjection to the Holy Roman Church; and the letter concluded with the assurance that the author had written not to attack others, but to defend himself, praying them at the same time no longer to shut their hearts to the truth. As Easter in the year 631 would have fallen, according to the Irish computation, on April 21, and according to the Roman on March 24, the council above-mentioned must have been held in 630, the return of the deputies would have been in 632, and Cummian's letter have been written in the following year.

In the same connection Pope Honorius addressed a letter to the nation of the Scots, in which, according to Bede, "he earnestly exhorted them not to esteem their small number, placed in the utmost borders of the earth, wiser than all the ancient and modern Churches of Christ throughout the world, and not to celebrate a different Easter, contrary to the paschal calculation and the synodical decrees of all the bishops upon earth." This letter bore fruit. "For," Bede goes on, "the Scots who dwelt in the southern districts of Ireland, by the admonition of the Bishop of the Apostolic See, learned to observe Easter according to the canonical custom." The northern Scots of Ireland, however, continued to retain their national customs. The distinction here drawn by Bede between the northern and southern provinces of Scots in Ireland is founded on the ancient traditional division of the island into two parts, Seth Mogha and Seth Cuina. To the southern district belonged Munster and part of Leinster, while the northern division contained the rest of Leinster, Ulster, and Connaught. Durrow, although founded by St. Columba, belonged to the southern province, and appears to have severed its connection with Iona and conformed to the Roman use.

Some years later a letter on the Easter question was dispatched by the Irish Church to Pope Severinus, who, however, died without replying to it. An answer was sent by his successor, John IV (640–642), exhorting them, among other matters, to the extirpation of the Pelagian heresy, which had been gaining ground among them. Bede gives us the opening of the letter which was addressed by the Pope elect before his consecration, together with other dignities of the Roman Church, to the bishops, priests, doctors, and abbots of the Scottish Church. Among these last appears the name of Segine, Abbot of Iona, which monastery was evidently ranked by the Pope as forming a part of the Irish Church.

In the year 635, Tighernach mentions the foundation of a church by Abbot Segine in the little island of Rathlin, off the north coast of Ireland; and in the same year occurred the death of Eochaidh, Abbot of Lismore.

King Oswy

Northumbria was for the next few years the scene of various political revolutions, in the course of which the virtuous king Oswald was defeated and slain by his mortal enemy, Penda the pagan king of Mercia, at the battle of Maserfeld, in Shropshire, on the 5th of August 642. Taken from his people in the flower of his age, after a reign of hardly nine years, Oswald carried to the tomb the reputation of one of the noblest monarchs and greatest benefactors of his kingdom, as of the Christian Church at large. He was succeeded on the throne by his brother Oswy, who reigned from 642 to 670. The first twelve years of his reign were occupied in constant wars with the ferocious Penda, who attacked Oswy's capital city, Bamborough in Bernicia, and laid it in flames. It would have been totally consumed had not Aidan, who perceived the conflagration from Lindisfarne, obtained by his prayers a change of wind, which drove back the flames upon the assailants and compelled them to retire. On the 15th of November 654, a battle was fought between the two princes, in which Penda was slain. Bede scarcely estimates highly enough the value of this victory, by which Oswy not only delivered his people from the danger of constant irruptions from Mercia, but also obtained for the latter country the incalculable blessing of Christianity. King Oswy also extended the bounds of his own kingdom. In the south he ruled Mercia for three years; in the north he overcame not only the Britons, but also the Picts and Scots. The dominion of the Angles over the Britons of Alclyde, the Scots of Dalriada, and the southern Picts, lasted for almost thirty years. The union of the southern Picts with Northumbria appears to have been brought about by some tie of kindred between the two royal houses; for at the time when Oswy overthrew the Britons and Scots, a prince of the royal family of Northumbria was reigning over the southern Picts. Tighernach calls him Talorcan, and records his death in 657. "It is probable," remarks Skene, "that Oswy claimed the submission of the southern Picts to himself as the cousin and heir to King Talorcan, and enforced his claim by force of arms." How far his dominion extended cannot now be decided with any certainty; but it probably included, at least nominally, the whole territory of the southern Picts, and embraced, at any rate, what Bede calls the province of the Picts immediately north of the Firth of Forth.

Oswy died in 670 and was succeeded by his son Egfrid, who reigned for fifteen years over the whole of Northumbria, including both Bernicia and Deira. This restless and warlike monarch—who in 672 took up arms against the revolted Picts, was in conflict with Bishop Wilfrid in 678, and six years later devastated a great part of Ireland with his army—was finally in the year 685 defeated and slain at the battle of Battle of Dunnichen, in the country of the southern Picts, which he had penetrated in order to their subjugation. This battle was of great political importance; for "from that time," says Bede, "the hopes and strength of the Anglic kingdom began to fluctuate and to retrograde, for the Picts recovered the territory belonging to them which the Angles had held, and the Scots who were in Britain, and a certain part of the Britons, regained their liberty, which they have now enjoyed for about forty-six years." The inhabitants of the little kingdom of Scottish Dalriada and the Britons of Alclyde ceased to be tributary to the Angles; while the Picts whose territory had been formally incorporated into Northumbria now regained their full political independence. The British provinces of Alclyde which became independent of the Angles were the modern counties of Dumbarton, Renfrew, Lanark, Ayr, and Dumfries, with the fortress of Dumbarton. The part over which the Northumbrian Angles continued to hold sway included the district of Galloway, with its Pictish population and its capital Whithern, and the territory lying between Galloway and the river Derwent, together with Carlisle. The political subjection of this district to Northumbria was necessarily accompanied by spiritual dependence also, which made itself felt to the close of the Middle Ages, and found expression in the claim of the Archbishop of York to jurisdiction over the Scottish episcopate.

Segine, Finan, Cummene, and Colman

Under Abbot Segine of Iona, another monk from the same renowned monastery in the person of the saintly Finan succeeded in 651 to the episcopal see of Lindisfarne. The community entrusted to him this important office in consideration of his piety and zeal. Finan was to complete in Northumbria what Aidan had begun. He erected a new church in Lindisfarne, not indeed of stone, for which skilled masons were wanting, but of oak, with an outer covering of reeds. He induced King Oswy to atone for the murder of Oswin, King of Deira, whom he had put to death on the 20th August, 651, by building churches and performing other works of piety. Oswin's remains were solemnly deposited in a chapel dedicated to the Blessed Virgin, and built on a lofty granite cliff near where the Tyne, the boundary between Deira and Bernicia, flows into the North Sea. Up to the Reformation this church was one of the most frequented places of pilgrimage in England. The ruins of seven great arches still rise against the sky and proclaim to the traveler, and still more to the sailor, the glory and the decay of the ancient faith. The pious Eanfleda, Oswy's wife, founded after his death, under the guidance of St. Finan, an important monastery on the spot where Oswin had perished; and Trumhere, of the royal house of Northumbria, but educated and ordained in Ireland, was appointed its superior. Finan's most remarkable foundation was the great monastery Streaneshalch, better known by its Danish name of Whitby. In thanksgiving to God for his great victory over Penda, he made over to the Abbess Hilda ten hides of land, situated on a precipitous headland on the coast of Yorkshire. Here at Streaneshalch—that is, the bay of the lighthouse—she erected the great convent which was to be not only a guide to mariners, but was to serve for centuries as a *pharos* of spiritual and religious life for the whole country. In place of the first monastery there arose in Norman times a new structure, whose ruins still speak to travelers of its departed grandeur. So strict was the religious observance of the nuns of Whitby that, says Cardinal Moran, "it became a proverb among the Northumbrians that the image of the primitive Church, where all things were common among the Christians, was to be seen realized there." Finan ended his laborious life in 660, after a nine years' episcopate, and was buried in his church of Lindisfarne. In the Aberdeen Breviary he is styled "a man of venerable life, a bishop of great sanctity, an eloquent teacher of unbelieving races, remarkable for his training in virtue and his liberal education. While he surpassed all his contemporaries in every manner of knowledge, as well as in circumspection and prudence, he chiefly devoted himself to good works, and presented in his life a most apt example of virtue."

The next successor but one in the abbacy of Iona to Segine, who died in 653, was Cummene, who held the office from 657 to 669. This period was signalized by a number of important events, which directly or indirectly had great influence in the development of the Scottish Church. As already mentioned, Oswy extended his rule to the southern Picts, the Britons of Strathclyde, and the Scots of Dalriada. On Finan's death another monk from Iona succeeded to the see of Lindisfarne. This was Colman, who attended the disputation at Whitby as defender of his national customs. In the same year in which Finan died is recorded also the death of Daniel, Bishop of Kingarth. Bede says of Finan that he was "ordained and sent by the Scots," but of Colman, that he was sent out of Scotia, or Ireland; and this, as Dr. Skene well observes, makes it highly probable that the bishops of Kingarth were called in to Iona to consecrate these Northumbrian missionaries; but Bishop Daniel having died, and his successor not yet being appointed, Colman had to betake himself to Ireland in order to obtain consecration.

The Synod of Whitby in 664

The most important event by far during Abbot Cummene's tenure of office was the Conference of Whitby, which was to have such momentous results for the Columban Church in Northumbria. Its immediate cause was the dispute that had been raised between the Scottish monks and certain priests who had come into Northumbria from Gaul or Italy. Hence there sprang up an antagonism which was embittered by some of the native clergy conforming to the Roman use. Conspicuous among these was Ronan, a priest, according to Mabillon, of Irish family, but who had spent a long period in the monasteries of Gaul. The discussions which he held with Finan only confirmed the latter in his adherence to his national customs. Under Colman, the successor of Finan, the controversy broke out with renewed vehemence. Queen Eanfleda, with her Kentish chaplain, Romanus, whom she had brought with her from her southern home, observed the Roman Easter, while the king followed the Scottish reckoning, in opposition to his son Alchfrid, who had been instructed in Christianity by the Abbot Wilfrid. The latter had received his early training at Lindisfarne, but had afterward repaired to Rome, where he devoted several years to the study of Holy Scripture, the Benedictine Rule, canon law, and the question of paschal reckoning. He also received the Roman tonsure. On his journey home Wilfrid spent three years with his friend Delphinus, Archbishop of Lyons, and then returned to England. The king bestowed on him the Abbey of Hrypon (Ripon), where he displayed an energy so unbounded and so abundantly blessed, that he was reverenced far and wide as an oracle. Agilbert, Bishop of the West Saxons, who was united by close friendship both with Prince Alchfrid and Wilfrid, proposed the holding of a synod for the settlement of the Easter controversy and other ecclesiastical questions. It was accordingly held in 664, in the monastery of Whitby. King Oswy and his son Alchfrid were both present. On the Roman side appeared Bishops Agilbert and Tuda, with Wilfrid, Agatho, James, and Romanus. On the Scottish side were Bishop Colman with his ecclesiastics from Ireland, Bishop Cedd of Essex, who had been educated and ordained in Ireland, and who acted as interpreter, and Abbot Eata with Abbess Hilda and her followers. It was remarkable that all the theologians present had received the greater part if not the whole of their training in the Irish or Scottish schools. Colman and Wilfrid were called upon by the king to lead the discussion, which is given at length by Bede. It was conducted chiefly by the young and ardent Wilfrid, and turned upon the question of the paschal computation, on the bearing of which a few observations will suffice.

Two questions are included in the controversy: first, What cycle of years must elapse before the Easter full moon would fall again on the same day? And secondly, On what day of the paschal moon Easter was to be celebrated—or, more precisely, When the fourteenth day of the paschal moon falls on a Sunday, is Easter to be kept on that day? For the paschal computation, the Roman Church followed, up to the sixth century, the cycle of eighty-four years. St. Patrick, when sent to Ireland by Pope St. Celestine I (422–432), introduced this use into his native country, where it still prevailed in the seventh century. The adoption of this cycle was meanwhile the source of various inaccuracies and variations between East and West, on account of which the introduction of a reformed cycle was proposed in Rome. The first alteration took place in 444, in which year Easter fell, according to the eighty-four years' cycle, on March 26, while the more accurate Alexandrine reckoning adopted in the East fixed it for April 23. Leo the Great was not yet inclined to propose a permanent change, but conformed to the Alexandrine computation for the current year. A similar step was taken in the year 455. Pope Hilary (461–468), the successor of Leo, had, while Archdeacon of Rome, directed Victor of Aquitaine to harmonize the Roman and Alexandrine calculations. But even his mode of reckoning, which accurately marked the new moons, did not altogether extinguish the differences between the two Churches. Pope Hilary appears to have adopted in 465, at the close of the eighty-four years' cycle, the reformed computation of Victor, which was followed by the Roman Church until 567. In this year Dionysius the Less drew up, on the basis of the nineteen years' cycle, a paschal table which put an end to all discrepancies, and established one and the same system of reckoning for East and West alike. Rome and the whole of Italy adopted this calculation, while Gaul retained the canon of Victor, and Britain still adhered to the cycle of eighty-four years, somewhat improved by Sulpicius Severus.

The Celtic computation, in the second place, included the fourteenth day of the paschal moon itself, if it happened to be Sunday, among the days on which Easter might be celebrated. The Celts differed essentially from the so-called Quartodecimans, who attached more importance to the day of the month than to that of the week, and consequently did not keep Easter exclusively on Sunday. The practice of the Celts was derived from the paschal table of Anatolius, Bishop of Laodicea in Syria, who had in the year 277 drawn up a new canon on the basis of the nineteen years' cycle, in which the 19th of March was considered as the vernal equinox. The Irish and British Churches had adopted this canon in a corrupted form. The practice in question had been, however, if not expressly, at least by implication, condemned, in their decree on the keeping of Easter, by the First Ecumenical Council of Nice.

With these preliminary remarks, we return to Synod of Whitby. St. Colman brought forward his case with self-command and dignity, and without the least exaggeration. "My usage is that which my predecessors followed, and all our fathers have done the same. They were men of God, and we are taught that their customs were handed down from St. John. In reverence for these holy men, I can and I will consent to no change. Our venerable tradition is that the fourteenth moon, if it fall on Sunday, is to be kept as Easter Day. Let the other side now give the grounds of their observance." Bishop Agilbert being unable, from his imperfect knowledge of English, to comply with King Oswy's request to enter the discussion, Abbot Wilfrid began. "We keep Easter," he said, "as we have seen it kept by all Christians at Rome, where the blessed apostles Peter and Paul lived, taught, suffered, and were buried. In Italy and Gaul, we are assured, the same practice is followed: Africa, Asia, Greece—the whole Christian world is on our side, notwithstanding all difference of language and of customs. Only these [Colman and his followers], with their allies in obstinacy, the Picts and the Britons, inhabiting the most distant parts of the earth, are acting foolishly in setting themselves against the whole world." "Strange indeed," was Colman's rejoinder, "that you should speak of that as foolishness, in which we do but follow the example of him who was thought worthy to lean his head on the breast of the Lord." Wilfrid endeavored to explain the supposed practice of St. John by the equally doubtful hypothesis that the apostle conformed to Jewish customs, adding that St. Peter had brought to Rome the true observance, which was now in use throughout the world. The Irish, he said, did not follow the old Asiatic custom, according to which Easter was kept even on a weekday, if it happened to be the fourteenth moon; and their position was therefore all the worse, as being opposed to the Jewish law and to the Gospel as well. On Colman appealing to the Canon of Anatolius, Wilfrid made a lengthy reply, in which he assigned to that bishop opinions of which, says Petavius, he had never dreamt. He then took the safer ground of authority, comparing St. Peter, prince of the apostles, to St. Columba, whose practice Colman had adduced in his own favor. "Is this Columba of yours," he cried—"nay, I will call him *our* Columba, in so far as he was Christ's servant, however holy or powerful by his virtues he may have been—is he to be preferred to the most blessed prince of the apostles, to whom the Lord said, 'You are Peter, and upon this rock I will build my Church, and the gates of hell shall not prevail against it; and I will give you the keys of the kingdom of heaven.'" At these words of Wilfrid, the king asked Colman, "Is it true that these words were spoken by our Lord to St. Peter?" "It is true, O king," was the answer. "Do you claim like authority as given to your Columba?" "No," replied Colman. "You are then agreed in this, that these words were said to Peter, and the keys of heaven were given to him by the Lord?" "Even so," they answered. "Then," so ran the royal decision, "I say to you, that this is the doorkeeper of heaven, whom I dare not gainsay; but as far as I am able, I desire in all things to obey him, lest, perchance, when I come to heaven's gate, there be none to open them for me, if he who keeps the keys be turned away from me."

From a review of the proceedings of the synod, it is clear that the impetuous Wilfrid was by no means happy in his arguments, so far as they rested on a historical basis; and even in his appeal to the authority of the Church, he could only, up to a certain point, enlist the Holy See and its practice on his side, for there was no question of any formal condemnation of the Celtic customs on the part of Rome. Still less could he, with any justice, appeal to Holy Scripture for proof of his statements. Besides, the discipline at that time observed in Rome with reference to the Easter festival had not been in use for more than a century. It was nevertheless intrinsically right, and on this ground should have commanded the adherence of the Scots, even in the absence of an express command of the Holy See. In consideration, however, of the fact that no such decision had been given, Colman thought fit to resign his see of Lindisfarne. When the members of the assembly had accepted the decision of the king, and had declared themselves ready to adopt the Roman Easter, he made known his resolution of departure, and betook himself back to Iona with his monks. In view of the fact that this act of Colman's was not followed by any rupture with the Holy See, no importance can be attached to the theory of some writers who have seen in Colman's departure a rejection of the authority of Rome. The bishop took with him from Lindisfarne a portion of the relics of St. Aidan, leaving the rest in the sacristy of the church. With him the Columban Church in the kingdom of Northumbria came to an end after an existence of thirty years. The portrait which Bede has left us of the departed Colman depicts him as a great bishop, an eloquent preacher, and a man of most amiable disposition, such as was calculated everywhere to inspire esteem and veneration for the ecclesiastical state.

According to Bede, Colman returned to Ireland. We learn, however, from other sources, that he did not do so for four years. Tighernach speaks of his settling in the little island of Inisbofin, on the west coast of Ireland, in 668. Before this, however, he went to Iona, where he reported to Abbot Cummene the result of the disputation at Whitby. The treatment which their common father St. Columba had received at the synod was doubtless the motive which induced Cummene to undertake the Life of the saint to which Adamnan refers, and which afterward served as the basis of his own work. Tighernach records the death of Cummene in 669, and with it that of two saints belonging to the Church of the southern Picts—Ithaman or Ethamanus of Madderty in Strathearn, and Corindu or Caren of Fetteresso in the Mearns.

Failbhe

The successor of Cummene was Failbhe, who held the abbacy for ten years, in the first of which Wilfrid became Bishop of York. His diocese, in consequence of the successful wars of King Oswy, included the territories of the southern Picts, the Britons of Strathclyde, and the Scots of Dalriada. Wilfrid received consecration in Paris. There is little doubt that the full influence of his zeal and energy as bishop was directed against the Columban Church with its strong national leanings. We are told by his biographer, Eddi, that "under him churches were multiplied both in the south among the Saxons, and in the north among the Britons, Scots, and Picts—Wilfrid having everywhere ordained priests and deacons, and governed new churches." The territories of the northern Picts, however, lying beyond the Grampians, remained subject to the Abbots of Iona as before. Under Abbot Failbhe the Columban monks made considerable advances northward. Maelrubha, of the race of the northern Hy-Neill, who was related through his mother to Comgall of Bangor, and had been trained in that monastery among the Irish Picts, came to Britain in 671, and two years later founded the church of Aporcrosan (Applecross) on the west coast, between Loch Carron and Loch Broom. Later on he planted churches also in the south and west of the Isle of Skye, and in Easter Ross and elsewhere. In the same year Failbhe went to Ireland, returning to Iona after a stay of three years. To this period also belongs the arrival of Comgan and his sister Kentigerna in the district of Lochalsh, where they built churches. Wilfrid Cummene lived to see the expulsion of Wilfrid from York by Egfrid, King of Northumbria, who in 678 drove the bishop from his see. The ground of this proceeding was Wilfrid's refusal to give his assent to a scheme for the partition of the diocese of York into four smaller sees, which was proposed by King Egfrid and Archbishop Theodore of Canterbury, and sanctioned by a synod.

Wilfrid appealed without delay to Pope Agatho, who convoked an assembly in Rome in 679 for the adjustment of the question. Wilfrid, as well as a representative of the Primate Theodore, took part in the proceedings, the upshot of which was that he was to be reinstated in his diocese and was himself to select bishops for the three new sees as his coadjutors, who were, however, to be consecrated by the Archbishop of Canterbury. In order to put an end to all disputes, and also to suppress the Monothelite heresy, John, abbot and precentor, was sent to England as legate. Wilfrid remained in Rome until 680, and took part in the Synod which was assembled by the Pope to name deputies for the sixth general council. Abbot Failbhe died in the previous year, and at the same time Tigernach records the death, in Aberdeenshire, of Neachtan Neir, venerated by the people under the name of Nathalan or Nachlan.

Adamnan, biographer of St. Columba

The progress of events has now brought us to perhaps the greatest of the Abbots of Iona next to Columba himself, of whom he has left us, in his biography of the saint, the most authentic particulars. Adamnan, born in 624, was descended from Conall Gubban, and belonged to the family of St. Columba. Under his abbacy Wilfrid's extensive diocese was divided by King Egfrid between Eata and Bosa; and a further partition followed three years later, by which the care of the southern Picts north of the Firth of Forth was assigned to Bishop Trumuin. When Egfrid, however, fell in 685 at the battle of Dunnichen, and his dominion over the Picts and Scots came to an end, Trumuin was forced to fly from his diocese. In the year 686 we find Adamnan on a visit to King Alchfrid, whom he had known in Ireland, and with whom he was on friendly terms. The object of his journey was to obtain the freedom of certain Irish prisoners whom Beret, the Northumbrian general, had captured in his expedition against

Ireland. The king granted the abbot's request, and Adamnan brought sixty of the captives back to their homes.

On his return to Iona, he sent to Lorn for oak wood in order to repair the monastery, and for this purpose procured no less than twelve shiploads of timber. In the following winter he entertained a somewhat noteworthy guest. Arculphus, a bishop of Gaul, who had gone to Jerusalem to visit the holy places, was driven northward by violent storms on his homeward voyage, and finally reached Iona, where he was hospitably received by Adamnan. During his stay at Iona, he gave the abbot much information as to the Holy Land, which Adamnan committed to writing and handed down to posterity.

A second journey of Adamnan to Northumbria in the year 688 was fraught with important results to the Scottish Church. The abbot became acquainted with the ritual observances of the Angles, and discovered that the customs of his country differed from those of the universal Church. He gave the preference to the latter; "for," says Bede, "he was a good and wise man, and most deeply learned in the knowledge of the Scriptures." Abbot Ceolfrid, in his letter to Naiton, king of the Picts, calls him "Adamnan, the abbot and renowned priest of the Columbans." On his return home, he was desirous of introducing the Roman rite among his monks, but he was unable to prevail over their opposition. In the following year died Iolan, bishop of Kingarth in Bute; and in 693 the body of the Pictish king, Brude mac Bile, was interred at Iona.

Four years later we meet with Adamnan again in Ireland, whither he was accompanied by Brude, king of the Picts. His object was to obtain the sanction of the Irish people to a law exempting women from the duty of rendering assistance in war. For this purpose a synod assembled at Tara, under the presidency of the Abbot of Armagh, and was attended by thirty-nine ecclesiastics and forty-seven chiefs of tribes. The law by which women were freed from the burden of *fecht* and *sluagad* was known as "*Lex Innocentium*," and the canons of the synod were called *Cain Adhamhnain* or "Lex Adamnani." During his sojourn in Ireland, Bede tells us, he explained to the people the proper time of celebrating Easter, converted many of them—and nearly all who were not subject to Iona—from their error, and brought them back to Catholic unity. On his return to Iona (after canonically celebrating Easter in Ireland), he urged upon his monks the Catholic observance. He did not live, however, to see his efforts crowned with success; for he died before the next year came round, on September 23, 704, in his seventy-seventh year. A collection of canonical decisions on the subject of the use of and abstinence from certain meats bears the name of Adamnan. It is generally held to have been published at the same time as the "*Lex Innocentium*," for both Ireland and Scotland.

A number of churches owed their foundation to Adamnan's apostolic labors. The friendly relations which he maintained with the Pictish kings were doubtless of great advantage to him in this respect. In the territory of the northern Picts he erected Forglen, on the river Doveran; while south of Drumalban he founded the monasteries of Dull and Glendochart. The last was dedicated to St. Fillan, whose name survives in Strathfillan; and in the Firth of Forth is Inchkeith, "over which presided St. Adamnan the abbot."

Schism on Iona

Adamnan was succeeded by Conmael, of the tribe of Airgialla in Ireland, but not, it is to be remarked, of the family of St. Columba. Three years afterward we meet with another Abbot of Iona, Duncadh, belonging to the tribe of the founder. After Conmael's death Bishop Ceode became abbot, and he was in turn succeeded by Dorbeni. At this time, however, Duncadh was still living. It is evident from this that a schism had broken out in Iona after Adamnan's death. The monks who were in favor of the Roman rite elected Conmael abbot, while the opposing party, after the lapse of three years, entrusted the office to Duncadh, of the kindred of the founder. On the Roman side was Naiton, king of the Picts, who, says Bede, "renounced the error which, with his people, he had hitherto held, and submitted with all his subjects to celebrate the Catholic time of the Lord's resurrection." At length, in 716, all the monks of Iona were persuaded to adopt the Roman rite, urged thereto by the earnest admonitions of Egbert, an ecclesiastic universally honored for sanctity and learning. In the daughter houses of Iona the opposition lasted long. The Columban monks in the various monasteries throughout the Pictish territory offered a stubborn resistance to the decrees of King Naiton, ordering the adoption of the Roman observance. The monarch had recourse to forcible measures; and Tighernach records that in the year 717, Abbot Duncadh being dead, and Faelchu in sole possession of the abbacy, the whole of the Columban monks were expelled from the country. "It is possible," adds Dr. Skene, "that the monks of the monasteries recently established among the southern Picts by Adamnan may have conformed; but those of the older foundations, such as Abernethy and *Cillrigmonadh*, or St. Andrews, were probably driven out; and thus, with the expulsion of the family of Iona, terminated the primacy of its monastery over the monasteries and churches in the extensive districts of the east and north of Scotland, which formed at that time the kingdom of the Picts."

CHAPTER 5

THE CHURCHES
OF CUMBRIA AND LOTHIAN

St. Kentigern (514–603)

The kingdom of Cumbria, or Strathclyde, with its capital Alclyde, or Dumbarton, extended from the river Clyde in the north to the river Derwent in Cumberland. It was inhabited by Britons, among whom St. Ninian had planted the faith in the fifth century. In the course of time, however, almost every trace of Christianity had disappeared, when, toward the end of the sixth century, a new apostle was raised up in the person of St. Kentigern. Just as Columba was the pioneer of religion among the northern Picts, so it was to Kentigern that the kingdom of Strathclyde, or Cumbria, owed the blessing of the faith. The literature of the subject is, unfortunately, very scanty: a detailed biography by the monk Jocelyn of Furness, with a fragment of another life, represents all that we know of St. Kentigern. The latter work dates from the time of Herbert, Bishop of Glasgow, who died in 1164, and who had filled the office of abbot of the monasteries of Selkirk and Kelso before he was consecrated bishop by Pope Eugenius III (1145–1153). At his instance, a foreign ecclesiastic, who had traveled much and become a "cleric of St. Kentigern," wrote a life of the saint, part of which only is extant, in an MS. preserved in the British Museum. It has been printed by Cosmo Innes in the *Registrum Episcopatus Glasguensis*, and forms the substance of the Lessons in the Aberdeen Breviary for the feast of St. Thenew, Kentigern's mother. A complete biography of the saint was written by Jocelyn, in the Cistercian monastery of Furness, in South Cumbria. It consists of forty-four chapters, and is dedicated to Jocelin, Bishop of Glasgow.

Kentigern was born about the year 514. His mother, Thenew, or Thenog, was of Irish family. Jocelyn calls her simply "the daughter of a very pagan king, who ruled in the north of Britain." According to the same biographer, the royal maiden was deceived and betrayed by an unknown suitor, and was in consequence condemned by the laws of her country to be cast down from the summit of a high rock called Kep-Duff. Receiving no injury thereby, she was then, by order of the king, placed in a small boat and sent out into the open sea. God, however, protected her. The skiff drifted on to the coast of Fifeshire, where St. Servanus, who dwelt there, received her, and where her son was born. Servanus instructed and baptized the mother and child, to whom he gave the name of Kyentyern (i.e., *Ceann-Tighearn*, meaning "lord and master"), for which, however, he afterward, in his great affection for the boy, substituted that of *Munghu*, or Mungo, signifying "the well-beloved." The mother of Kentigern, who became renowned for her life of holy penance, was afterward commemorated as a saint in the Scottish calendars. A chapel was built upon the spot where she had given birth to Kentigern, and where the ruins of a medieval church are still pointed out. A church was also dedicated to her in Glasgow; and though it was demolished at the Reformation, her name still survives in St. Enoch's Square and the great railway terminus and hotel erected there.

With regard to St. Servanus, it has been already pointed

out that his supposed connection with Kentigern, as related by Jocelyn, involves an anachronism of more than a century. The ancient and still extant Life of Servanus, which makes him the founder of the monastery of Culross, contains not the slightest indication in support of the statements of Kentigern's biographers, or the belief of popular tradition.

Arrived at manhood, Kentigern crossed the Firth of Forth and established himself at Cathares, now called Glasgow, where many disciples soon gathered round him: We read that he built his cell beside the cemetery, which he planted with trees; and as late as the year 1500 the "trees of St. Kentigern" are mentioned as landmarks in the deeds of the city of Glasgow. The distracted state of religion in Cumbria at this time rendered very desirable the appointment of a bishop. At the desire of the king and clergy, Kentigern received episcopal consecration in 540, a bishop being sent for to Ireland to officiate on the occasion; and he at once commenced with the greatest zeal his apostolic labors. His biographer relates many interesting details of his life, and portrays him as a bishop full of the love of God and of his fellow men, deeply practiced in mortification, and distinguished by God with many wonderful gifts.

The saint was not, however, exempt from his share of suffering. A tyrannous prince named Morcant had ascended the throne of Strathclyde, and not only scoffed at the life and teaching of the holy man, but openly opposed him, attributing his miracles to diabolic agency. In consequence of this persecution, Kentigern retired for a time to Menevia, in South Wales. On his way thither he turned aside to Carlisle, called by the Romans Lugorallium, and by the Angles Luel, or sometimes, from its fortifications, Caer-luel. It was, from Roman times, one of the most important places in the north of Britain, and famous for its splendid buildings, of which extensive remains were still standing in the days of Bede. Here Kentigern preached the Gospel to its heathen inhabitants, and erected a cross near the city, on a wooded spot which was thence called Crossfield (now Crossthwaite). In the middle ages a noble church was built there, dedicated "to the name of blessed Kentigern." Eight other churches in Cumberland still bear the saint's name. From Cumberland Kentigern proceeded down the eastern coast of England to the monastery of Menevia, or St. David's, in Wales, where its holy founder received him with joy and veneration.

Meanwhile circumstances had greatly changed for the better in Strathclyde. Rederech, surnamed Hael, or the Bountiful, who succeeded to the throne in 573, devoted himself to the restoration of the Christian religion in his kingdom. A battle was fought at Ardderyd between Christians and pagans, in which the former obtained the victory. Rederoch at once invited Kentigern to return to his native land, and himself went forth to welcome him. The king and the bishop met at Holdelm, now Hoddam, in Dumfriesshire. A great multitude were present, and Kentigern addressed them in a long discourse, in which he dwelt on the main features of paganism, and exhorted them to root it out of the land. Three points he specially referred to. First, that the elements were not to be adored, for the origin of their existence was not within but without themselves, God having made all material things for man's service out of nothing. Secondly, the worshiping of idols was no less prohibited: as the work of human hands they deserved rather to be consumed by fire than to receive divine honors. Thirdly, Woden, the deity whose worship the Angles had introduced, was no divinity, but a mere mortal man, ancestor of one of their tribes, who had descended into the grave like every one else.

In Holdelm, Kentigern fixed his temporary residence, and thence he made many missionary journeys. He preached among the Picts of Galloway, and also in the kingdom of the southern Picts, beyond the Firth of Forth. The statement of Jocelyn, however, that the saint sent missionaries to "the Orcades, Norway, and Ysalanda," or Iceland, is opposed to the probably trustworthy account of the Irish geographer Diciul, who flourished at the beginning of the ninth century, and according to whom the earliest missionaries to the northern islands all came from Ireland. After a time Kentigern returned to Glasgow, where he is related to have worked many wonderful miracles. One of these, the discovery of the queen's ring in the mouth of a salmon, is still commemorated in the arms of Glasgow, which bear a salmon with a ring in its mouth.

In connection with St. Kentigern, we once more come across the great figure of St. Columba. A meeting is recorded to have taken place between the apostle of Northern Caledonia and the holy bishop of Cumbria. As the latter did not probably return to his diocese before 582, this meeting would in all likelihood be about 584, in which year Columba was laboring in the country about the Tay, and so was near the kingdom of Strathclyde. The two saints met, accompanied by a great following of their disciples, amid prayers and spiritual songs. They embraced, gave each other the kiss of peace, and then exchanged their pastoral staves. That of St. Columba was long preserved in St. Wilfrid's monastery at Ripon, where it was held in high honor on account of the sanctity both of him who gave it and of him who received it.

Jocelyn gives a remarkable account of Kentigern's death—it probably reports the tradition of the Church of Glasgow. "When the Octave of the Lord's Epiphany, on which the gentle bishop himself had been wont every year to wash a multitude of people in holy baptism, was dawning, the man of God entered a vessel of hot water, which he had first blessed with the sign of salvation. And when he had been some little time in it, bowing his head as if sinking into a calm sleep, he yielded up his spirit." This was on January 13, 612. His body probably rests on the spot where now stands the beautiful cathedral of Glasgow. The bell brought by the saint from Rome was renowned in the middle ages. It was tolled through the city every evening, to invite the prayers of the citizens for the souls of the faithful departed. The feast of St. Kentigern was kept by the Scottish Church on January 13. The Bollandists give a proper Mass for the festival, dating from the thirteenth century; and the Advocates' Library in Edinburgh has acquired a breviary belonging to the same period, and containing a proper Office of the saint.

Of the fortunes of the see of Kentigern in the period immediately following his death, nothing is accurately known, excepting the fact that Sedulius, *"episcopus Britanniae de genere Scotorum,"* who attended the council held at Rome by Gregory II in 721, was probably one of his successors. The authentic history of the see of Glasgow begins with the appointment of Bishop John by King David I about the year 1115. From the *Inquisitio*, held on this occasion by royal command, we learn that Kentigern had had several successors, and that certain estates, anciently the property of the see, but of which it had been plundered, were now restored to it.

St. Cuthbert (626–687)

As St. Kentigern may be called the founder of Christianity in Strathclyde, so the Church of Lothian honors as its apostle the illustrious St. Cuthbert. Of several Lives of this saint which have come down to us, the one with the greatest claim to authenticity is that written by Bede, not more than forty years after Cuthbert's death. In this respect he has been more fortunate than the other saints of the Celtic Church. It was not for hundreds of years that St. Ninian found a biographer in Aelred of Rievaulx, and even Columba's Life was not written till he had been dead for more than a century. But the biography of Cuthbert was the work of the most famous and learned writer of the Anglo-Saxon

Church, one whose life was in part contemporary with his own. Bede tells us that he had shown his manuscript to Herefrid the priest, and to other persons who were thoroughly acquainted with the life of the man of God, in order that they might correct or expunge what they thought right. He conscientiously adopted their suggestions, and only then, he says, ventured to commit to parchment the result of his careful researches. Curiously enough, Bede gives us no information as to the birth and parentage of Cuthbert. He presents him to us in boyhood, "keeping watch over his flocks on distant mountains." These mountains, according to the anonymous Life of the saint, were the hills of Lammermoor, where Cuthbert tended his master's herds on a height near the river Leader. It was here, Bede tells us, that he saw in a vision the holy Bishop Aidan borne to heaven by angels. He thereupon resolved to embrace the religious life, and at once set out for the monastery of Melrose, where Boisil received him and gave him the tonsure. As St. Aidan died in 651, this incident gives us the first certain date in Cuthbert's life.

The Surtees Society has edited a valuable tract on the birth of St. Cuthbert, from the MSS. of the chapter of York, according to which the saint was of Irish origin, his mother, Sabina, being of royal blood, and his father the King of Connathe, who took Sabina captive, and after slaying all her relatives, sent her to his own mother, who gave her shelter, and with her entered a convent. Here Cuthbert was born and baptized, receiving the Irish name of Mulluch. He was subsequently taken by his mother to Britain. The question naturally presents itself, on what ground Bede abstains from all mention of Cuthbert's birth and parentage. Considering the fact that they were almost contemporaries, he cannot be supposed to have had no knowledge of the circumstances in question; and Dr. Skene conjectures that the current tradition on the subject may have been one of those portions of the biography which Herefrid and the rest considered of doubtful authenticity, and which Bede in consequence expunged. However that may be, the Irish birth of the saint appears to have been the tradition of the Church of Durham. The date of his birth can only be approximately ascertained. We know that Cuthbert resigned the bishopric of Lindisfarne in 686, and died in 687. If by Bede's expression that he had then "reached old age" we understand that he was about sixty (he could hardly have been less), this would place his birth at about 626. As already mentioned, he entered in 651 the monastery of Melrose, where he spent ten years in the most exact observance of the holy rule.

Eata, Abbot of Melrose, received in 661 a gift of forty hides of land at Ripon, on which to found a monastery. Among those sent to the new foundation was Cuthbert, who was appointed to the office of guest-master. It was during this period that he was one day found worthy to entertain an angel in the guise of a pilgrim, who, at his departure, left with the saint three loaves, "such," writes Bede, "as this world cannot produce; excelling the lilies in whiteness, the roses in perfume, and the honey in sweetness." The stay of Cuthbert at Ripon, however, was short. Even before the Synod of Whitby, the viceroy of Deira, the southern province of Northumbria, had abandoned the Celtic observance and summoned the monks of Ripon likewise to adopt the Roman use. On their refusing to do so, they were forced to leave Ripon and returned to Melrose. It was then that Cuthbert began those missionary labors, so abundant and so fruitful, which his biographers cannot find words to praise. For a time he led the life of a hermit, near the village of Dull, in Atholl. On the summit of a hill in the neighborhood he built a cell, and at his prayer a stream of water gushed from the rock. The spring now bears the name of St. Dabi's Well, for St. Dabius also lived here in after-times. At the foot of this hill soon after St. Cuthbert's death, Adamnan built a monastery, around which rose in later ages the town and University of St. Andrews. From the lay abbot of this monastery in the eleventh century descended the royal house of Stuart. Bede relates many incidents illustrating the great austerities practiced by St. Cuthbert at this time. Among others he was wont to recite the entire Psalter while standing in ice-cold water.

About the year 660 England and Ireland were visited by a pestilence known as the *Buidhe Conaill,* or Yellow Plague, which wrought terrible ravages among the people. Among others, Boisil, Prior of Melrose, fell a victim to it. He was succeeded by St. Cuthbert, who fulfilled the duties of his new office with such zeal and fervor (according to Bede's expression) as became a saint, and presented to the community the shining example of a perfect religious man. His missionary labors extended over the territory of the southern Picts, as well as the Niduari Picts in the district of Galloway. His zeal in the preaching of the Word of God was indescribable, and thousands flocked to him for the relief of their consciences, and to benefit by his teaching and counsel.

The result of the Conference of Whitby opened a wider field for St. Cuthbert's activity in the service of God. Bishop Colman, as we have seen, resigned his see and betook himself back to Iona. Abbot Eata, however, with his prior Cuthbert, gave in their adherence to the Roman use, and Eata was placed over the monastery of Lindisfarne, which he committed to the care of Cuthbert. The saint was earnestly desirous that his cause of Community should conform to the customs of Rome. A few for a time held out; but he overcame their opposition, says Bede, "by the modest power of patience; and by daily efforts he brought them little by little to a better frame of mind." Colman's successor in the see of Lindisfarne was Tuda, who had been consecrated bishop among the southern Picts of Ireland.

In the year 676, when Cuthbert had been twelve years Prior of Lindisfarne, he resolved (as was not unusual in those times) to withdraw from the monastery, and to lead a life of solitude, of which, Bede tells us, he had already begun to learn the rudiments. A few miles to the south of Lindisfarne, and about two miles from the mainland, lies the little group of seven islets known as the Farne Islands. On one of these Cuthbert fixed his abode; and here he built what, according to Bede's description, appears to have been one of those beehive-shaped cells, of which remains still exist in many parts of Scotland. The solitude, however, which he had desired so ardently was to be his only to a limited extent; for not only were the monks of Lindisfarne wont to visit him on certain festivals of the year, but pilgrims came to him from all parts of England and Scotland to ask for his prayers and counsel in their difficulties. A number of legends connected with the saint's life on these solitary islands lingers in Northumberland even to the present day.

While St. Cuthbert thus lived apart from the world, great changes were taking place in the Northumbrian Church. Bishop Tuda, "a good and religious man," as Bede calls him, having been taken from his flock by the pestilence, King Alchfrid, as we have already seen, sent Abbot Wilfrid of Ripon to Gaul, where he received consecration. While he was still absent, King Oswy sent Chad, Abbot of Lastingham, to Kent, to be there consecrated bishop of the see of York. The Archbishop of Canterbury having just died, Chad was consecrated by Vini, Bishop of Wessex, assisted by two other British bishops, who followed the Roman rite. On Wilfrid's return from Paris, however, Chad was translated to the episcopate of Mercia, and Wilfrid from the year 669 to 678 held the see of York, in the now greatly extended kingdom of Northumbria. During his episcopate, as we learn from Eddi, Wilfrid's biographer, he founded, on land given by Queen Ethelreda, the famous Abbey of Hexham, on the Tyne, and dedicated it to St. Andrew, in memory of a visit which he had made many years before to a church of that apostle in Rome, to pray for the gift of rightly understanding the Gospel and rightly preaching it to the people. Numerous churches were afterward dedicated to the same apostle, both in Northumbria and the country of the southern Picts. A few years after the foundation of Hexham, King Egfrid (the successor of Oswy), who had long cherished resentment against Wilfrid, procured his deposition; and his see was divided into two new dioceses. Bosa, a monk of Whitby, became Bishop of Deira, the southern province, with his see at York, and Abbot Eata of Hexham, or, according to some authorities, of Lindisfarne. Three years later, a further subdivision took plaice, two more bishoprics being erected. Tunbert was appointed to Hexham, Eata to Lindisfarne, and Trumuin to the province of the southern Picts, at that time subject to the Angles. Wilfrid, as we have seen, appealed to Rome, and was reinstated in his see by a council held there in 679. On his return to England, however, he was seized by Egfrid and imprisoned for nine months. The efforts of the saintly Abbess Ebba, aunt to the king, procured his liberation, only, however, on the condition of perpetual banishment from Northumbria. He took refuge in Sussex, where he converted by his preaching the still heathen inhabitants; and it was not till 687, King Egrid being dead, that Archbishop Theodore obtained his restoration to his see.

For eight years St. Cuthbert had lived his life of solitude on the island of Farne, and the fame of his sanctity and wisdom had spread far and wide. Tunbert of Hexham had for some reason been deposed from his see; and at a synod held at Twyford in the year 684, in presence of King Egfrid and under the presidency of Archbishop Theodore of Canterbury, Cuthbert was unanimously chosen to the vacant bishopric. On Easter Sunday of the following year he was consecrated by Theodore at York, in the presence of the king and seven bishops. At his own wish, Lindisfarne, where he had lived as a monk, was, "with the assent of King Egfrid, and of the archbishop and these seven bishops, and of all the magnates," assigned to Cuthbert as his see, while Eata returned to Hexham. The king granted to him at his consecration the district of Cartmell, "with all the Britons who dwelt upon it"; and his jurisdiction was extended westward to Carlisle. On the 20th of May 684, he made his entry into the ancient Roman town, whose inhabitants came out to meet him in solemn procession, and conducted him to the city fountain, "the wondrous work of Roman hands." Scarcely had they arrived here, when suddenly Cuthbert appeared almost overcome with emotion. Leaning on his pastoral staff, he seemed hardly able to stand erect. For a while he remained silent; then, looking up to heaven, he exclaimed, "Even now is the contest decided." A few days later his words were verified by the tidings of Egfrid's disastrous defeat at Dimnichen by the southern Picts, whose territory he had invaded against the advice of the holy and prudent bishop.

An object of St. Cuthbert's especial solicitude was the pastoral supervision of the monasteries of nuns, of which there were several in his diocese. He spent some time at Coldingham, imparting to its community instruction in the spiritual life; and he labored, as we are told, both by word and example, so that the perfect harmony between his life and his teaching was an edification to all. The monastery of Whitby was at this time governed by Elfleda, a niece of King Oswald. St. Cuthbert, who cherished a deep devotion for the saintly founder of Lindisfarne, frequently visited Whitby, in order to assist the abbess by his wise counsels in the administration of her responsible office.

The saint spent the festival of Christmas 686 with the monks of Lindisfarne, and immediately afterward withdrew once more to his hermitage at Farne. When the brethren questioned him as to what day he would return, he answered, "On the day when you shall bring back my dead body to your monastery." Soon after the New Year of 687, he became sensible that his end was approaching. He directed the brethren to wrap his body, after his death, in the linen which the Abbess Verca had given him, and to bury it, as they so earnestly desired, in their church at

Lindisfarne. "Keep peace one with another," were his last words to the community, "and ever guard the divine gift of charity. Maintain concord with other servants of Christ. Despise not any of the household of faith who come to you seeking hospitality, but receive and entertain and dismiss them with friendliness and affection. And do not think yourselves better than others of the same faith and manner of life; only with such as err from the unity of Catholic peace have no communion." These were Cuthbert's last words. He died on March 19, 687, and his remains were taken to Lindisfarne, where amid the prayers and solemn chants of the brethren they were interred in a stone sarcophagus on the right of the altar in St. Peter's Church. Eleven years afterward the body, still uncorrupt, was taken from the tomb, wrapped in fresh linen, and placed in a shrine of wood, which was laid on the floor of the sanctuary.

Henceforward, in the Celtic and Northumbrian Churches alike, St. Cuthbert continued to be honored with the highest veneration. King Alfred the Great invoked him in his struggle against the Danes, and received from him in a vision the promise of victory and liberation for his people. King Canute made a pilgrimage barefooted to his shrine, and William the Conqueror brought costly offerings and laid them on his tomb. It was beneath the banner of St. Cuthbert that the Anglo-Normans won their most brilliant victories. The British Museum still boasts a memorial of the holy bishop, in the magnificent copy of the Gospels which bears his name, and which is considered one of the principal gems of ancient Celtic art. To his memory is dedicated the cathedral of Durham, where his relics were placed in the twelfth century—a truly magnificent monument of the zealous piety of the proud Anglo-Norman race. York and Canterbury may present the most perfect development of the English Gothic architecture; but the Norman style, as we see it at Durham with its imposing masses, its colossal pillars, and its ornamentation recalling the intricacies of Celtic or Eastern art, at once awes and enchants the beholder, and inspires him with a deep sense of his dependence on a higher power. The sanctuary of Durham was not spared in the whirlwind of the Reformation. When, in 1537, the shrines of the cathedral were plundered by command of Henry VIII, the body of St. Cuthbert was found to be still incorrupt. The tomb was again opened in 1827, when a skeleton and other remains were discovered, which Mr. Raine, the librarian of the cathedral, who was present at the investigation, believed to be those of the saint.

Developments in Northumbria

It was not long after St. Cuthbert's holy death that Adamnan made his second visit to Northumbria. The resolute adherence of the late saintly bishop to the Roman rite had no doubt considerable influence in inducing the Abbot of Iona to abandon, as we have seen he did, his national customs for those of the Roman Church. Through his efforts, as Bede tells us, many of the Scots in Ireland, and also of the Britons, were won over to the same observance. The Britons here alluded to are those of Strathclyde, who had lately succeeded in throwing off the Saxon yoke; for the Britons of North Wales did not conform until the year 768, nor those of South Wales until 777. The Bishop of Strathclyde at this time was probably Sedulius, the same who attended the Council at Rome in 721, and subscribed its canons.

The see of Lindisfarne, rendered vacant by St. Cuthbert's death, was filled by the appointment of Bishop Wilfrid, who had by this time been restored to favor by King Alchfrid. Wilfrid died in 709, and was interred on the south side of the altar in St. Peter's Church at Ripon—a man of lofty ideals, and zealous to enthusiasm for the glory of God and the authority of the Holy See, of unblemished life, profound piety, wide attainments, and an inflexible sense of justice that no influence could turn aside.

Wilfrid was succeeded in the bishopric of Hexham by his friend and disciple Acca, of whom Bede tells us that, "being a man most active, one to do great things in the sight of God and of men, beautified the fabric of his church, which was dedicated to blessed Andrew, with various ornaments and wonderful works. For he took great pains, and does so still, to procure from all parts relics of the apostles and martyrs of Christ, and to erect altars for their veneration; and also collecting with the greatest industry the history of their sufferings, with other ecclesiastical works, he formed a large and noble library." Among these relics were, without doubt, those of St. Andrew, and among the histories would be the Acts of the same apostle. When Bede finished his *History* in 731, Acca still occupied the see of Hexham. Wilfrid (the second of the name) was at the same time Bishop of York, Edilweld of Lindisfarne, and Pecthelm of Whithern (Candida Casa), "which," adds Bede, "having been lately erected into an episcopal see on account of the increase in the numbers of the faithful, has him for its first bishop." The district of Strathclyde had thrown off the Northumbrian yoke, but Galloway still remained subject to the Angles, who, a few years before the completion of Bede's history, had restored, as he mentions above, the ancient see of St. Ninian, which in course of time had fallen into decay. It was occupied, up to the year 803, by five bishops in succession, and to this period belongs the devotion to St. Cuthbert and St. Oswald in Ayrshire and Galloway, and the dedication of numerous churches in their honor. Toward the end of the eighth century Galloway was overrun by the Picts and Scots, and with their assistance the inhabitants broke off from Northumbrian rule. The last bishop of the Anglo-Saxon see was Beadwulf, who assisted at the coronation of Eardwulf, King of Northumbria, in 795, and died in 803.

At about this period may be placed the foundation of the celebrated monastery of Tyninghame. With the breaking up, in the year 681, of the diocese of York, its connection with the Churches of Lothian and Cumbria came to an end. The diocese of Lindisfarne, however, extended to the Firth of Forth. Simeon of Durham records in the year 756 the death, in Tyninghame, of the anchorite Balthere, popularly known as "St. Baldred of the Bass." Bower erroneously associates this saint with Kentigern, from whom he was removed by more than a hundred years; Alcuin, who wrote in the eighth century, clearly connects him with the Bass. The diocese of Lindisfarne contained, besides Tyninghame, the monasteries of Melrose, Edwinesburgh (Edinburgh, where still exists St. Cuthbert's Church), and Abercorn, on the southern shore of the Firth of Forth, the monastery where Trumuin resided when bishop of the southern Picts, and whence he fled after the disastrous battle of Dunnichen.

CHAPTER 6

THE CULDEES
AND THE SECULAR CLERGY

End of the monastic period

The monastic period of the Scottish Church came to a close at the beginning of the eighth century. In the place of the Columban monks, expelled, as we have seen, from the Pictish dominions in 717, we find the Culdees appearing on the scene. The name of Culdee meets us for the first time in the eighth century. "To Adamnan, to Eddi, and to Bede," says Skene, "it was utterly unknown. They knew of no body of clergy who bore this name, and in the whole range of ecclesiastical history there is nothing more entirely destitute of authority than the application of this name to the Columban monks of the sixth and seventh centuries, or more utterly baseless than the fabric which has been raised upon that assumption. Like many of our popular notions, it originated with Hector Boece [author of the *Scotorum Historia*], and, at a time when the influence of his fabulous history was still paramount in Scotland, it became associated with an ecclesiastical controversy which powerfully engaged the sympathies of the Scottish people; and this gave it a force and vitality which renders it difficult for the popular mind to regard the history of the early

118

Scottish Church through any other medium." By adopting these erroneous views, the Reformers of the sixteenth century found (as it was obviously their interest to do) an apparent warrant for their doctrines in those of the earliest Christianity of the country; and they met with the more credence, since for the period in question trustworthy guidance, such as that afforded by Adamnan and Bede for the preceding century, is unfortunately wanting. The history of the Scottish Church from the eighth to the eleventh century is involved, for the most part, in profound obscurity; and it is not until the reign of Malcolm Canmor and Margaret (who, like their son David I, applied themselves to the erection of bishoprics and to the foundation of monasteries for the various religious orders), that light begins to break in upon it.

There were two distinct agencies instrumental in bringing about an alteration in the constitution of the Scottish Church: on the one hand, the formation of a secular clergy; on the other, the appearance of the Culdees. The former came from without, the latter was an outgrowth of the monastic Church itself. The introduction of the secular clergy originated with Wilfrid of York, the champion, as we have already seen, of the Roman Easter reckoning; but the immediate occasion of the change was the expulsion of the Columban monks from Pictland by King Nectan, in 717, on their refusal to conform to the custom of Rome.

The legend which treats of this revolution in the Church of Scotland is preserved in the Aberdeen Breviary, in the lessons assigned to the Feast of St. Boniface. Harmonizing as it does with the narrative of Bede, and corroborated as well by the dedications of the churches connected with it, some account of the legend in question cannot be omitted here.

Boniface was born in Bethsaida, of Israelitish origin. In his thirty-sixth year he received priest's orders from the Patriarch of Jerusalem. When forty-six years of age he went to Rome, where he became bishop and cardinal, and was finally raised to the Papal chair. Calling some of his brethren into his oratory, he informed them of his intention to send forth a mission to the ends of the earth, impelled thereto by the love of God and of those peoples who dwelt on the confines of Europe. "Send," was their answer, "religious men, even as your predecessors Celestine and Gregory sent Palladius, Patrick, and Augustine." Boniface, however, rejoined that he had been commanded by St. Peter, in a vision, himself to undertake this mission. Accordingly, after the requisite preparation, he set out from Rome, accompanied by Benedict, Servandus, Pensandus, Benevolus, Madianus, and Principuus, all of whom were of episcopal rank. Besides these, there followed Boniface the Abbesses Crescentia and Triduana, together with seven priests, deacons, sub-deacons, acolytes, exorcists, lectors, and doorkeepers, and a great multitude of God-fearing men and women. On their arrival at the Firth of Forth, they were met by King Nectan, who, with his nobles, received the sacrament of baptism at their hands. The king dedicated to the Holy Trinity the spot where he had been baptized, and made it over as a free gift to Boniface. The saint at once commenced his apostolic labors—"wrote a hundred and fifty books, erected the same number of churches, with as many bishops, and a thousand priests. He converted to the faith of Christ and baptized thirty-six thousand men and women; and in the eighty-fourth year of his age, on the 16th day of March, full of grace and of virtue, departed to Christ." According to another form of the legend, his name was Albanus Kiritinus, surnamed Bonifacius.

There is an evident connection between this legend and the proceedings taken by King Nectan against the Columban monks in his zeal for the introduction of the Roman customs. Among those who took part in the Irish Synod presided over by Adamnan in 697, we find the name of *Cuiritan epscop*, or Bishop Kiritinus. Irish and Scottish alike commemorated the saint on the same day, the 16th of March. Kiritinus of the legend, and the Irish bishop of that name, thus appear to be identical. The substance of the legend is undoubtedly historic, and gives us the true origin of the substitution of the secular clergy for the expelled monks.

The legend of St. Fergusianus, or Fergus, belongs to the same period. He came from Ireland, founded three churches in the west of Scotland; and after laboring at the conversion of the people of Caithness, he built a basilica (which still exists) at Lungley, and died at a great age in Glamis. Here are still to be seen a cave and a well bearing his name; and an old tradition that his head was taken to Scone, and reverently kept there, is confirmed by an entry in the books of the Lord High Treasurer of Scotland, of the payment by James IV (1488–1497) for a silver case to contain the relic in question.

No fewer than fourteen churches in the east of Scotland were dedicated to St. Peter. According to the Irish annalist Tighernach, the religious enthusiasm of King Nectan led him, in the year 724, to enter the ecclesiastical state; and he probably retired to the church which he had had built by Northumbrian architects in the Roman style, and had promised to dedicate to St. Peter. This was in all likelihood Restennot or Rosemarkie. There may be some foundation for the conjecture that the king sought reconciliation with the monks of Iona, and found in that island a last resting place. An old burial place there still bears the name of Cill-ma-Neachthan.

Christian hermits

Besides the external influence of which we have spoken, there was another, developed within the pale of the Church itself, which contributed greatly to the change that took place at this period in the ecclesiastical organization of Scotland. From the earliest Christian centuries, the life based upon the fulfillment of the evangelical counsels had been of a threefold character.

Thus St. Jerome speaks of three kinds of monks: Cenobites, leading a common life; Anchorites, who lived apart from men, each one by himself; and finally, those called *Remoboth* whom he describes as of evil and abandoned life. Cassian also, who was of Scythian extraction, recognizes three sorts of monks— Cenobites, Anchorites, and Sarabaites. The latter lived in small companies of two or three together, without following any fixed rule. Cassian looks on this last as a degenerate form of monastic life. There is still another kind of monk which he describes, composed of those who, unable or unwilling to bear the yoke of community life, retired to separate cells, in emulation of the Anchorites, without, however, sufficient fervor or perseverance to imitate their virtues. In the nineteenth Conference, a certain Abbot John, who had abandoned the eremitical life and entered a monastery, is questioned as to the respective advantages of these two modes of life. The purport of his answer is that the life of a hermit is suitable only for such as have attained a very high degree of spiritual perfection. St. Isidore of Seville also bears testimony on the point. He, too, speaks of Cenobites, who, in imitation of the Christians of apostolic times, sold all that they had and led a life in common; of hermits, who, taking Elias and John the Baptist as their models, gave themselves up to perfect solitude and a supernatural contempt of the world; and finally, of Anchorites, who, having attained to a high degree of perfection in the cenobitical life, shut themselves up in separate cells, and devoted themselves entirely to the contemplation of heavenly things. So also Venerable Bede, himself a master of the spiritual life, alludes to these different kinds of monks. In his History he tells us how St. Cuthbert "proceeded to the adoption of a hermit life of solitary contemplation and secret silence," and in his Life of the saint the same thought finds expression: "He was now permitted," he says, "to ascend to the leisure of divine contemplation, and rejoiced that he had reached the lot of those of whom we sing in the Psalm: 'The saints shall go from virtue to virtue: the God of Gods shall be seen in Sion.'" The truth was, in short, recognized and acted upon, that the more a man can detach himself from material things, the closer will be the union of his soul with God. This was the principle on which the eremitical life was based.

Deicolae, Coledei, or Keledei

The hermits, whose lofty aspirations to religious perfection were manifested in the mortification and devotion of their lives, were known by the distinguishing name of *Deicolae*, or worshipers of God, in the highest sense of the term; while the ordinary body of the faithful were called *Christicolae*, or worshipers of Christ. St. Athanasius, Bishop of Alexandria, the warm friend and promoter of Western monachism, mentions in his Life of St. Anthony that "his neighbors, and the monks whom he visited, called him *Deicola*; and, using terms of natural affection, loved him, some as a son, others as a brother." So, too, Bishop Martin, who styles himself "Scotus," speaks in a letter to Miro, King of Galicia, about the year 560, of "those arduous and perfect rules which are observed by a few most excellent *Deicolae*." And Columbanus, the celebrated propagator of monasticism in Eastern Gaul, thus portrays the truly religious man: "Whosoever wishes to become a dwelling place for God, let him strive to make himself humble and quiet, that not by fluency of words and suppleness of body, but by the reality of his humility, he may be known as a true *Deicola*."

It was the almost inevitable result of the natural weakness of humanity that a life so absolutely isolated as the eremitical should be exposed to various dangers, and become the occasion of abuses and excesses. We find, in consequence, many attempts made by ecclesiastical authority in the seventh and eighth centuries to bring the solitaries together, and to subject them to conventual discipline. The Council of Toledo, held in 646, permitted only well-instructed monks to live the life of recluses. The forty-first canon of the Council of Trullo (692) enacted that those desiring to live as solitaries must have first passed three years in a monastery; and the forty-second canon ordered that such hermits as came into the towns in black dress and with long hair, and associated with seculars, must be compelled to enter a monastery and to wear the monastic habit, otherwise they were to be expelled from the towns.

In the following century we find similar, but more systematic, efforts to bestow upon the hermits the benefit of regular observance. The well-known rule of Chrodigang, Bishop of Metz, contains thirty-four chapters of instructions for the community life of his clergy. These were primarily intended only for the clergy of Metz: the hermits were not at first affected by them, nor were they in force in other dioceses. The advantages, however, of the new canonical life were soon widely appreciated, and the rule of Chrodigang made its way throughout the Church. In its extended form, it consists of eighty-six chapters, of which the eighty-first treats directly of the so-called *Deicolae*, with the object of binding them to canonical life. It is in the form of the letter of brought a certain Deicola, "sent in the name of Christ to canonical the priests and clerics, for their instruction and exhortation"; and the author addresses himself "to the beloved priests of Christ's Churches, the bishops and all the clergy everywhere therein, and their servants, and to all the *Deicolae* living in the whole world." He exhorts them to live uprightly and piously, and especially to show due obedience to their superiors, as becomes servants of God. Finally, the observance of the canonical rule is strictly enjoined them. At the General Council held at Aix-la-Chapelle in 816 and 817, the rule of Chrodigang was adopted, and a number of canons were enacted, relating to the details of the canonical life.

In Britain and in Ireland, as well as on the Saxon Continent, we early meet with the *Deicolae*. The Peterborough MS. of the Anglo-Saxon Chronicle, in the account of the monastic foundation at that place in 655, refers to God-fearing monks— *Godefrihte*, evidently the Saxon equivalent of *Deicolae*. A council held in Northumberland in the year 687 ordered that all canons should live canonically, and all monks and nuns according to monastic rule. "That the title of God-worshipers," observes Skene, "passed down to the canon clerics, at least to those who lived separately, appears from this: that when King Athelstan was on his march against the Scots in 936, he halted at York, and there besought of the ministers of St. Peter's Church, who were then called *Colidei*, to offer up their prayers on behalf of himself and his expedition. They are said to be 'men of holy life and honest conversation, then styled Colidei, who maintained a number of poor people, and withal had but little whereon to live.'" "These *Colidei*" says Dr .Reeves, "were the officiating clergy of the cathedral church of St. Peter's at York in 946, and discharged the double function of divine service and eleemosynary entertainment." The word *Colidei* is, in fact, merely an inversion of *Deicolae*, the name by which these canon clerics were known in other parts of Christendom.

If we turn to Ireland, we shall find there the development, at a very early period, of the same form of ascetic life. It often happened that the abbot or one of the brethren of a monastery retired for a certain time to a separate cell, in order to give himself more entirely to prayer and penitential exercises. During this period he held no intercourse with the other brethren. The cells erected for this purpose were built of stone, without mortar, with thick walls and dome-shaped roofs, something in the form of beehives. They bore the name of *carcair*, or prison cells. Those who devoted themselves to such a solitary life were considered as giving themselves absolutely up to God, and were hence known as *Deoraidh*, or "God's pilgrims." Their connection with the monastery, however, was not thereby severed; on the contrary, when the abbacy became vacant, the *Deoradh De*, or pilgrim, was entitled, according to ancient Irish custom, to succeed in the fifth place. It is, moreover, prescribed by the Breton laws, that if a bishop be found guilty of certain offenses, the *Ferleginn* or lector shall succeed to the bishopric, and the bishop shall go into the hermitage, or pilgrimage of God.

The ancient Catalogue of the Saints, which throws so much light on the early history of the Irish Church, ends in 666, the year of the great pestilence. After this period we find the appellations of the Continental anchorites appearing in Irish form, similar to that bestowed on the Irish hermits themselves. Instead of the term *Deicolae*, which had hitherto been applied to them, we find them now designated as *Ceile De*. As *Christicola* becomes in Irish *Celechrist*, so *Deicola* takes the form of *Ceile De*. Dr. Skene shows, by a reference to a poem in the *Leabhar Breac* (part 2, p. 261), attributed to St. Mochuda, who died in 636, that these *Cele De* were not, strictly speaking, monks, as Reeves assumes. The sixth section of this poem treats "of the occupations of a monk," and the seventh "of the *Cele De*, or clerical recluse," thus clearly distinguishing one from the other. The connection, on the other hand, between the *Cele De* and the *Deicolae* of the Continent is unmistakable. The former, like the latter, were anchorites; for if any one bore the title of *Cele De*, it was only on the ground of his having lived as a solitary. Thus Angus the Culdee, the famous hagiologist, founded a desert called after his name. Again, the *Cele De*, like the *Deicolae*, are called the "people of God." The Annals of Ulster relate that in 921, "Armagh was pillaged on the 10th of November, the Saturday before St. Martin's Day, by Gofrith, grandson of Ivar, and his army, who saved the houses of prayer with their people of God, that is, *Cele De*, and their sick, and the whole church town, except some houses which were burned through neglect."

Like the *Deicolae*, too, the *Ceile De* of Ireland were brought, early in the ninth century, under canonical rule. This important fact is found in the form of legend—in which, however, the historical germ is easily detected. The Irish Annals record, under the year 811: "In this year the *Cele De* came over the sea with dry feet, without a vessel; and a written roll was given him from heaven, out of which he preached to the Irish; and it was carried up again when the sermon was finished." The date of the coming of this *Cele De* was sixty-eight years after Chrodegang drew up his canonical rule; it was subsequent also to the publication of the letter addressed by a certain *Deicola* to the *Deicolae* all over the world, and only five years before the Council of Aix-la-Chapelle. The legend above quoted may therefore be reasonably interpreted to refer to the introduction into Ireland of the canonical rule.

The *Cele De*, as they were called in Ireland, were known in Scotland as *Keledei*. Some account of their first appearance in the latter country is given—albeit obscurely—in the legend of St. Servanus or Serf. Its chief features are as follows. "Obeth, son of Eliud, was King of Canaan, and his wife was Alpia, daughter of a king of Arabia. The blessing of children, long denied to them, was at length vouchsafed by God in answer to their prayers and alms-deeds. Two sons were born to them, of whom one was named Generatius, and the other Malachias or Servanus. The name of Servanus was given him in baptism by Magonius, Bishop of Alexandria, in token of his especial dedication to God's service. After many wanderings he went to Rome, where for seven years he occupied the Apostolic Chair. Thence he traveled through Gaul and England to Scotland; and here he was met by Adamnan, the famous Abbot of Iona. He afterward visited Adamnan at Lochleven, and was shown by him an island in the lake, well adapted for the foundation of a religious house. "Here," remarks Skene, "we have the same journey to the west, the same occupation of the Papal throne, as we found in the legend of Boniface. This feature seems to characterize the legends of those missionaries who promoted the great change by which a new order of clergy, under the influence of the Roman Church, superseded the Columban monks in the eastern and northern districts of Scotland."

A still older Irish document—the tract on the mothers of the saints, attributed to Angus the Culdee—connects St. Servanus more closely with the west. According to this, "Alma, the daughter of the King of the *Cruithnech*" or Picts, "was the mother of Serb or Serf, son of Proc, King of Canaan, in Egypt; and he is the venerable old man who possesses Cuilenros, in Stratherne." In this form the legend assumes a distinctly Scottish character; Alpia, the daughter of an Arabian king, becoming Alma, daughter of the King of the Picts. The chronology of this account is consistent with the history of the period. Brude, the Pictish king in question, may be identified with the Brude who reigned from 697 to 706, and preceded Nectan, who expelled the Columban monks from his kingdom. The same King Brude appears in one of the chronicles connected with Lochleven; and at the same time the chronicler adds, "as St. Servanus came to Fife." In the chartulary of St. Andrews we find reference to a grant of the isle of Lochleven, by King Brude, "to Almighty God, and to St. Servanus, and to the Keledei hermits dwelling there, who are serving, and shall serve God, in that island."

We know, moreover, that Adamnan, who was so closely connected with St. Servanus, maintained the friendliest relations with Brude, and died in 704, only two years before him. It is evident, from what has been said, that St. Servanus could have had no connection, as was afterward held, with St. Kentigern, since we have undoubted evidence that his labors belong to the end of the seventh century, and not to the fifth or sixth. The first establishment of hermits, or *Keledei* in Scotland was that founded by St. Servanus, at the beginning of the eighth century; and Jocelyn of Furness is guilty of as great an anachronism in assigning the *Keledei* to the time of St. Kentigern, as in stating that St. Servanus was his teacher.

Foundation of St. Andrews

Reference must here be made to the legends relating to the foundation of St. Andrews, and its connection with St Andrew the Apostle. The legend is extant in two separate forms, of which we give the chief features. The first bears this title: "How it happens that the memory of St. Andrew the Apostle should exist more widely in the region of the Picts, now called Scotia, than in other regions; and how it comes that so many abbacies were anciently established there, which now in many cases are by hereditary right possessed by laymen." The legend relates the acts and martyrdom of St. Andrew, and tells how Regulus, a monk of Constantinople, brought the relics of the apostle to Scotland, where he met Ungus, son of Urguist, the King of the Picts, at a place called Mordurus. Ungus gave this place to God and to St. Andrew, that it should be the head and mother of all the churches in the country of the Picts. Here Regulus led a life of monastic holiness, having under him a third part of the land of Scotia, which he divided into abbacies. On account of the convenience of its situation, and the pleasantness of its localities, this place recommended itself to Picts, Scots, Danes, and Norwegians, who came to plunder the island. The first part of this legend, which treats of the martyrdom of St. Andrew at Patras, in Achaia, is authenticated by ecclesiastical history. The other portions are evidently derived from different sources: there is little connection between them, and they are inconsistent with one another, more especially in those parts relating to the bringing of the apostle's relics to Scotland.

The second form of the legend traces its origin to St. Andrews itself, and is of a more elaborate character. It states that in the year 345 Constantine collected a powerful army in order to invade Patras and avenge the death of St. Andrew; that before his entry into the city, Bishop Regulus was commanded in a vision to conceal certain of the relics of the saint; and that Constantine, on the city being taken, caused the sarcophagus, with the remaining relics, to be brought to Rome. The second part of this legend is simply a more elaborate and detailed version of the second part of the other. The Pictish King Hungus defeats his enemy, Athelstane, King of the Saxons, through the intercession of St. Andrew, whom the Picts, in consequence, vow to hold in honor forever. Three days after the battle, Bishop Regulus is bidden by angels to sail northward with the apostle's relics, and to build a church in his honor at the spot where his vessel happens to be wrecked. After many wanderings they are cast ashore on the eastern coast of Scotland, at a place formerly called Muckros, but now Kyrlimont. Here (where St. Andrews grew up in later times) Regulus erected a cross which he had brought from Patras; and King Ungus gave the place to God and St. Andrew, His apostle, as a gift forever. The names of thirteen Pictish witnesses of royal blood are given, taken apparently at random from the list of Pictish kings. The second legend closes thus: "These are the names of those who brought the relics of St. Andrew to Scotland: Regulus himself, the deacon Gelasius, Malthaes the hermit . . . and seven hermits from the island of the Tiber."

A comparison of these two legends shows the different part assigned to Regulus in each. In the first he appears in Scotland as a simple monk; in the second, he is concerned, as Bishop of Patras, with the removal of the relics thence: in one he founds abbeys in Scotia, of which he possesses a third part; in the other, he is represented as a bishop, with priests and deacons among his followers, and as founding churches dedicated to St. Andrew. The first legend, in a word, bears a thoroughly monastic stamp; the second deals with a secular clergy. The older legend, therefore, takes us back to the monastic Church of St. Columba, and we find, in fact, the name of Regulus in the records of that period. After the synod of Drumceitt, in the year 573, which was attended by Columba and Aidan, King of Dalriada, the former founded the church of Drumcliffe, near Sligo. He was met on this occasion by the chief ecclesiastics of the neighborhood, among whom was Riagail, or Regulus, of Muicinis, whose name appears in the Irish martyrologies on the 16th of October. Regulus of St. Andrews is commemorated in the Scottish Calendar on the 17th of the same month; and we notice further, that while the name of the Irish Regulus's foundation is *Muicinis*, or Isle of Swine, the former name of Chilrymont, or St. Andrews, is said to have been *Muicross*, or the Promontory of Swine. "It seems, therefore," observes Skene, "to be a reasonable conclusion that the Regulus of Muicinis, commemorated on the 16th October, and the Regulus of Muicross, on the 17th of that month, were the same person, and that the historic Regulus belongs to a Columban church founded among those which Columba established among the southern Picts during the last years of his life."

Further corroboration of the older legend is afforded by the short but important reference which it contains to the passing of monastic property into lay hands—a state of things attributed in the legend to the successive depredations of the Picts, Scots, Danes, and Norwegians. This undoubtedly refers to the change which took place after the expulsion of the Columban monks in the beginning of the eighth century. Bede has testified as to what was the condition of affairs in Northumbria after that event. His well-known letter to Archbishop Egbert contains a long series of bitter lamentations over the decline of the Northumbrian Church, and the extensive spoliation of ecclesiastical property—a state of things all the more intolerable from the fact that the lay abbots made a pretense of continuing to keep up the monastic institutions. "As you yourselves well know," he writes, "those who are utterly regardless of monastic life have got into their power so many places under the name of monasteries, that there is no place at all which the sons of the nobility or of veteran soldiers may occupy." So elsewhere he says, "There are others guilty of a still more grievous offence. For, though they are themselves laics, and neither habituated to nor actuated by the love of a regular life, yet, by pecuniary payments to the kings, and under pretext of founding monasteries, they purchase for themselves territories in which they may have freer scope for their lust . . . and though they are themselves laymen, yet they have monks under their rule—or, rather, they are not monks when they assemble there, but such as, having been expelled from the true monasteries for the crime of disobedience, are found wandering up and down."

The melancholy picture here drawn by Bede of the state of the Northumbrian Church after the departure of the Columban monks seems to correspond with the title of the older legend of St. Andrew, given above. It was in the year 717, twelve years after the death of King Aldfrid of Northumbria, that Nectan expelled the Columban monks from his kingdom, and secular clergy were introduced in their place. The same results no doubt followed the change as we have seen in Northumbria; the monasteries fell into the hands of the tribes, or of individuals, and continued to preserve the semblance and nomenclature of religious houses, although the reality had disappeared. The motive for this, according to Bede, appears to have been the desire to preserve the right of immunity and similar privileges possessed by these foundations.

The foregoing investigations have cleared the way to our better understanding of the legend relating to the bringing of St. Andrew's relics to Scotland. If, as we have seen, the historic Regulus belongs to the period of the ancient Columban Church, the fictitious Regulus and the reception of the relics by King Hungus must be brought down no less certainly to a much later period. Hungus or Angus, King of the Picts, reigned from 731 to 761, and is noted for his expedition against the kingdom of Dalriada. Bede tells us that in the year 710 King Nectan placed his kingdom under the protection of St. Peter, and the national veneration for St. Andrew must therefore be of later date. Notwithstanding the fictitious antiquity of the legend, some notion of its true date seems to have been preserved; for we read in one chronicle[9] that in the year 761 "ye relikis of Sanct Andrew ye Apostel com in Scotland"—a date which corresponds with the last year of the reign of the King Angus (Mac Fergus) mentioned in the legend. If, then, the relics were brought into Scotland at this time, the further question presents itself, Whence did they come? It is certain that they were not brought immediately from the East, and there is more than a probability that they came from the monastery of Hexham. The church of Hexham, indeed, seems to have in several respects prefigured, as it were, the church of St. Andrews. Both were dedicated to St. Andrew; both possessed relics of that apostle. Wilfrid, as we know, founded Hexham in 674, and his successor Acca, who held the see from 709 to 732, brought thither the relics of St. Andrew. Wilfrid dedicated the church to the apostle, in gratitude for having received the gift of eloquence in preaching the Gospel, in answer, as he believed, to his prayers offered in the church of St. Andrew in Rome. He founded, besides, two chapels in honor of the Blessed Virgin and the Archangel Michael, through whose intercession he had recovered from a mortal sickness. So, if we turn to St. Andrews, we find it dedicated to the same apostle, and in possession of a portion of his relics; and, as at Hexham, we find there churches dedicated to the Blessed Virgin and to St. Michael. All this cannot but indicate a close connection between the two.

---

9. William Forbes Skene, *Chronicles of the Picts and Scots*, p. 387.

The Culdees of Scotland

The hermits, or Culdees, of Scotland, appear to have been brought under the canonical rule about the beginning of the ninth century, under King Constantine, son of Fergus, who reigned over the Picts from 790 to 820. He was the founder of the church of Dunkeld, where, according to Alexander Mylne, a canon of that church in 1575, "he placed religious men, commonly called *Keledei*, or *Colidei*—that is, worshipers of God—who, according to the rite of the Oriental Church, had wives, from whom, however, they lived apart while ministering, as was afterward the custom in the church of St. Regulus, now St. Andrews." Wyntoun, Prior of Lochleven, calls these Keledei *chanownys seculare*, or secular canons.

The result of our inquiry may be thus briefly summed up. The Culdees sprang from those ascetics who devoted themselves to the service of God in the solitude of separate cells, as the highest form of religious life, and who were styled *Deicolae*. In the course of time they formed themselves into communities of anchorites or hermits. They were clerics, and might be called monks, but only in the sense in which anchorites bore that name. Their first appearance in Scotland dates from about the same period as the introduction of the secular clergy, and they succeeded the Columban monks who had been driven from the Pictish kingdom, over the Drumalban mountain-range. Finally, in the ninth century, they were brought under the canonical rule, and in course of time the name of Culdee became almost synonymous with that of secular canons.

The view of certain writers, who would see in the institution of the Culdees some kind of organization opposed to the universal Catholic Church, is, as is evident from what we have said, perfectly untenable. Equally unfounded is the later theory of Ebrard, maintaining the identity of the Culdees with the Columban monks. So far, indeed, were they from being identical, that it was only the decline and final disappearance of the Columban Church that made way for the introduction of the Culdees into Scotland.

CHAPTER 7

IONA IN THE EIGHTH
AND NINTH CENTURIES

Picts and Scots, Danes and Norwegians

The political history of Scotland from the beginning of the eighth to the middle of the ninth century is taken up with continual wars between Picts, Angles, and Scots; with invasions of Danes and Norwegians, and their ravages in Northumbria, the west of Scotland, and the Hebrides; and finally, with the union of the Scots of Dalriada and the various Pictish races into one kingdom under the scepter of King Kenneth MacAlpine in the year 844.

"There is no more obscure period," observes Skene, "in the annals of the northern kingdoms, than the latter part of the eighth and the first half of the ninth centuries, and no more difficult question than to ascertain the nature and true character of that revolution which placed a Scottish race in possession of the kingdom of Scone. For this period we lose the guidance of the great Anglic historian Bede, and of the Irish annalist Tighernac. When we refer to trustworthy sources of information, we can find no record of any revolution at this time. They exhibit to us only the great confusion into which these kingdoms were thrown by the incessant depredations of the Norwegian and

Danish piratical hordes." Kenneth sprang, on his father's side, from the royal house of Dalriada, while by maternal descent he was of Pictish race. Various circumstances combined to favor the success of his claim to the throne of the Picts. The incursions of the Danes made a closer union between Picts and Scots almost a necessity; the old Pictish law of succession had in course of time almost broken down under Anglic influence; and finally, the foundation of Dunkeld had (as we shall see later) restored to the Columban clergy a certain influence in the country, which would doubtless be exercised in favor of a Scottish claimant to the Pictish crown.

The two immediate successors of Kenneth, his brother Donald (860–864), and his son Constantine (864–877), do not appear to have found themselves able efficiently to protect the kingdom from the dreaded Danes. Simeon of Durham tells us that in 875 the Danish host divided itself into two bands, one of which, under Halfdan, ravaged Northumbria and destroyed the Picts of Strathclyde. At the same time the north of Scotland was invaded by Thorstein the Red, son of Olav the White, the Norwegian King of Dublin. Caithness and Sutherland, Ross and Moray, "more than half Scotland," are said to have been subject to him for a year, until he was "betrayed by the Scots and slain in battle." Constantine himself, however, fell by the hands of the Danes. Driven from Ireland by the Norwegians in 877, they penetrated into Scotland by the Firth of Clyde, and in a battle fought at Inverdovet, in Fife, they defeated and slew the Pictish king. It is on this occasion that the name "Scotti," or Scots, is applied in the Pictish chronicle, for the first time, to the inhabitants of Pictland, instead of exclusively, as heretofore, to the people of Ireland or of Scottish Dalriada.

The ecclesiastical history of Scotland in the eighth and ninth centuries is involved, to great extent, in the same obscurity as we have already observed to characterize the political history of the period. The few detached and isolated facts which are recorded in the chronicles of the time afford little more than a bare outline of the history of the Scottish Church during these two centuries.

Two parties on Iona

As regards the monastery of Iona, so long the central point of religion in the country, we find it by this time in a state of transition. The Roman customs had, it is true, been adopted, but the rival parties in the monastery continued to uphold their respective views. We shall see again in force the nomination of the abbots according to the ancient system of tribal classification, and finally, the incursion of the Danes and the destruction of the monastery.

If, as we have seen, the Angles in the seventh century had to thank the Scottish Church for their saintly Bishop Aidan, it was, on the other hand, Egbert, a Northumbrian priest, who afterward brought Iona into closer union with Rome, and it was his efforts which procured the adoption of the Roman rites in the headquarters of Scottish religious life. "It appears," is the comment of Bede, "to have been a wonderful dispensation of the Divine goodness that the same nation which had wittingly, and without envy, communicated to the people of the Angles the knowledge of the true Deity, should afterward, by means of the same people, be brought, in those points wherein they were defective, to the rule of life." Bede adds that it was under Abbot Dunchad, about eighty years after they had sent Aidan to preach to the Angles, that the monks of Iona adopted the Catholic rites. It was about the year 710 that Egbert, who had long lived in Ireland in banishment for Christ's sake, and was renowned for his knowledge of the Scriptures and the perfection of his life, came among the monks of Iona and prevailed upon them to abandon the Celtic customs. They were by no means unanimous, however, in the adoption of the Roman use, and part of the community long preserved an attitude of opposition. According to Tighernach, the Catholic Easter was adopted in 716, but the coronal tonsure was not introduced till two years later. The expression of the Irish annalist seems to imply that it was forced on an unwilling community. The brethren were thus divided at this time into two parties, who gave expression to their rival views, as occasion offered itself, by their choice of abbots. We may designate them as the "national" and the "Catholic" parties.

On the death of Abbot Dunchad, in 717, Faelchu was left sole abbot of Iona. He was of the race of Conall Gulban, and his succession was in full accordance with the ancient law which prevailed in the monastic Church. We may suppose that the banishment of the Columban monks from the Pictish kingdom at this time was not without influence on the state of affairs at Iona. Many of the fugitives, doubtless, crossed over to Ireland, but others would betake themselves to Iona and add strength to the national party in that monastery. Bede's account of Egbert's last days and death at Iona, where he had spent thirteen years, seems to imply that the anti-Roman party was still stronger than might be inferred from his statements elsewhere. On the 24th of April 724, he tells us, Egbert celebrated the festival of Easter, in accordance with the reckoning of Rome; and on the same day he departed this life. "He rejoiced," says Bede, "to have continued in the flesh until he saw his followers admit and celebrate with him as Easter, the day which they had ever before avoided. Thus the most reverend father, being assured of their correction, rejoiced to see the day of the Lord; and he saw it and was glad." As a matter of fact, we find in 722, although Faelchu was still alive, another abbot, named Feidhlimidh, appearing on the scene. So on the death of Faelchu in 724, Cillene Fada succeeds to the abbacy, and he is in turn succeeded, in 726, by Cilline Droichteach, although all this time Feidhlimidh still remains abbot also.

Egbert did not therefore live to see the end of the schism. His efforts in this direction were supplemented by those of Sts. Ronan and Modan, who appear to have come from the south at about this time. An Abbot Modan is commemorated in the Scottish Calendars on February 4, and a bishop of the same name on November 14. Probably the same Modan is referred to in both places. St. Ronan's name occurs (as bishop) on February 7. A number of churches were dedicated to them, and the memory of Ronan is preserved in Iona by Port Ronan.

The year 726 was memorable for the appearance, while Feidhlimidh was still living, of an anchorite as abbot of Iona. Tighernach records that in 727, after the death of Cillene Fada, the relics of Adamnan were taken to Ireland, and his "*Lex Innocentium*" was revived, exempting women from military service. By the relics of Adamnan, however, appear to be understood, according to an ancient Brussels MS., the relics collected by him during his lifetime. "Illustrious was this Adamnan," so runs this document. "By him was gathered the great collection of the relics of the saints into one shrine; and this was the shrine which Cilline Droichteach, son of Dicolla, brought to Erin, to make peace and friendship between the Cinel Conaill and the Cinel Eoghain." Tighernach records the death, in 752, of Cilline Droichteach, "anchorite of Iona." He was not of the race of Conall Gulban, the legitimate successors to the abbacy, but of the southern Hy Neill. The fact that he took Adamnan's relics to Ireland, in connection with the renewal of the Law of the Innocents—a law associated with the period of Adamnan's conformity to Rome—identifies him likewise with the Roman party. We thus find at Iona similar results of the long Easter controversy to those we have already seen among the Picts—the introduction, not only of secular clergy, but also of anchorites, who now appear as forming one of the parties in Iona.

It is at this period that we first find applied to the abbots of

Iona a designation long known in Ireland. This is the title of *Comharba*, or co-arb, an Irish word signifying co-heir, and connected with the ancient law of succession to the abbacy. In Ireland, grants of land made to monastic foundations, were held to be personal gifts to the founder of the monastery. If the founder and the granter belonged to the same tribe, the representatives of the latter appointed a properly qualified person to the abbacy, in the event of its falling vacant; if they belonged to different tribes, the abbot was chosen from the tribe of the founder. The successors of the saint in the abbacy were styled his co-heirs, as inheriting the temporal and spiritual rights attached to the office. "When," observes Skene, "the integrity of the monastic institutions in Ireland began to be impaired in the seventh century, under the influence of the party who had conformed to Rome, the heads of the religious houses found it necessary to fall back more upon the rights and privileges inherited from the founders; and hence in this century the name of co-arb, in connection with the name of some eminent saint, came to designate the bishops or abbots who were the successors of his spiritual and temporal privileges, and eventually the possessor of the land, bearing the name of abbot, whether he were a layman or a cleric." Thus St. Gregory the Great is styled co-arb of the Apostle Peter—that is, Bishop of Rome. In the year 606 is recorded the death of Sillan, son of Caimin, Abbot of Bangor and co-arb of Comgall, the founder of that monastery. In 737 the Abbot of the Columban monastery of Apuorcrosan (Applecross) is termed the heir or co-arb of Maelruba, who founded it; and, on the same principle, the abbots of Iona bear the title of "co-arbs Columcille."

With the death of Abbot Slebhine, who held the office from 752 to 767, the schism in Iona appears to have come to an end; for he was the last abbot of the family of the great founder. A period of more than a century elapsed before another of the race of Conall Gulban succeeded to the abbacy. The absorption of

Scottish Dalriada into the Pictish kingdom no doubt contributed to the extinction of the rights of the tribe of the patron
saint, and tended to weaken the opposition of the national party.
From the year 767 there is no indication of any further schism
in the community.

From 772 to 801 Iona was governed by Breasal, who appears
to have been fully acknowledged by the Irish monasteries; for
we find in 778 Donnchadh, King of Ireland, and chief of the
northern Hy Neill, enforcing the law of Columcille in associa-
tion with Breasal as Abbot of Iona. During his term of office,
two Irish princes retired to Iona and died there—Niall Frosach,
formerly king of all Ireland, and Airtgaile, son of the King of
Connaught.

The Danes devastate Iona

In 794 is recorded the appearance of more unwelcome guests.
The Danes, or Gentiles, as the Annals term them, overran the
country, and in 795 Iona was devastated by their savage hordes.
Breasal was spared the sight of the destruction of his monastery.
He died in 801, and in the following year the monastery was
burned down by the Danes. Four years later occurred a still
heavier disaster. The whole community, numbering sixty-eight,
were slaughtered by the Danes, Abbot Cellach, son of Conghaile,
who Abbot appears to have fled to Ireland, alone escaping.

The monastic buildings of Iona at this time dated from the
abbacy of Adamnan, and were constructed of wood. The ruth-
less hand of the invader had entirely demolished them; and the
work of destruction was not confined to the monastery alone; the
whole island, so far as it had been in the course of time brought
under cultivation by the monks, had been reduced to a heap
of ruins. In any case, it offered no sufficient protection against
the recurrence of such attacks. On this account Abbot Cellach
appears to have resolved to transfer the mother-house of Iona

to Ireland. Shortly after the great disaster at Iona, the building of a new stone monastery was commenced at Kells, in Meath. On its completion in 814, Cellach resigned the office of abbot, and was succeeded by Diarmicius.

It appears to have been between the years 802 and 807 that the relics of St. Columba were removed and carried to Ireland. From the narrative of Adamnan we learn that the body of the saint had been enclosed in a stone coffin, and buried in a grave prepared for it. At the time Bede wrote his history (in 735) Iona still possessed Columba's relics; but in the year 807, to which the Book of Armagh belongs, they were preserved at Saul Patrick in county Down, in Ireland. The ancient custom of enshrining the bodies of the saints was at this time prevalent in the Irish Church. It had sprung up as one result of the closer union of Ireland with the center of Christendom, with the object of affording not only greater facility for the translation of the relics in case of war or other disturbance, but also a sort of warrant for enforcing the privileges of the monastery of which the saint was the founder. A detailed account of the enshrining of the remains of St. Cuthbert has come down to us from the pen of his biographer, Bede. Eleven years after the saint's death his body was taken from the stone sarcophagus in which it had been laid and deposited in a "light shrine," which was placed on the same spot, but above instead of below the pavement. A similar course was no doubt followed with regard to the relics of St. Columba. The Irish Annals record, toward the middle of the eighth century, the enshrining (the word used is *commutatio* or *positio*) of the relics of many saints: for example, in 733, of those of St. Peter, St. Paul, and St. Patrick; in 776 of St. Ere and St. Finnian of Clonard; in 784 of St. Ultan; in 799 of St. Conlaid, first bishop of Kildare; and in 800 of St. Ronan. Cogitosus, in his life of St. Bridget, describing the church of Kildare, says, "In it the glorious bodies both of Bishop Conleath and of this virgin

St. Bridget repose on the right and left sides of the altar, placed in ornamented shrines decorated with various devices of gold and silver, and gems and precious stones, with crowns of gold and silver hanging above them."

In the year 816, the Anglo-Saxon bishops held a council at Celchyth, south of the river Humber, under the presidency of Archbishop Wilfrid of Canterbury. The fifth canon of this council interdicts Scottish ecclesiastics from administering the sacraments, or performing other priestly functions in England, partly from a doubt as to their orders, partly because they were subject to no metropolitan. These two grounds of objection were, in fact, closely connected. It resulted from the monastic character of the Scottish Church that the bishops, who were few in number, and lived in the monasteries, had no proper jurisdiction; and they had probably fallen into some irregularities with regard to the administration of holy orders. The proper witnesses may have been wanting; or, again, there may have been some doubt as to their own consecration. A council held at Châlons-sur-Saone in 813 had already refused to recognize the validity of Scottish orders on similar grounds.

Rebuilding Iona in stone

In the hope that nothing more was to be feared from the Danes, Abbot Diarmaid brought back the shrine of St. Columba to Iona in the year 817. His first care was the rebuilding of the monastery, which was constructed on a more protected site, and the shrine of the saint was deposited in the new church, built of stone. But it was not long before they were overtaken by fresh disasters, at the hands of their old enemies. In the year 825 the Danes again attacked the monastery, which was at this time presided over by the pious Blathmac. Walafrid Strabo, his contemporary and biographer, tells us that he was a man of illustrious family, who early in life had renounced worldly honors and wealth, and embraced the religious state. On the approach of the Danish hordes, he summoned the brethren, and addressed them in the true martyr spirit. "Seek, my comrades, within your own minds, whether it be your determination to endure with me the coming fate, for the name of Christ. Whoever of you can face it, I pray you, arm yourselves with courage." No consideration would induce him to guide the rapacious pirates to the spot where the precious shrine of St. Columba was concealed. "Where the gold which you seek," he said, "may be hidden, I know not; but if it were permitted to me to know, never would the secret pass my lips." He was instantly cut to pieces.

In the year 829, Abbot Diarmaid, who appears to have meanwhile returned to Ireland, brought back to Iona the *Mionna* of St. Columba. The word *Mionna*, according to Dr. Reeves, signifies articles of veneration, such as the crosier, books, or vestment of a saint, upon which oaths were accustomed to be administered; while the word *Martra* denoted the actual relics or body of the saint. Thus Adamnan records a procession made by the brethren round a field, carrying the tunic of St. Columba, and a book written by his own hand, with the object of averting the evil effects of a long drought. About the year 829, then, the brethren who had escaped after the martyrdom of Blathmac were reassembled at Iona; and to this period no doubt belongs the construction, over the spot where the relics of St. Columba had been concealed, of a small chapel, whose foundations are still to be seen.

Abbot Innrechtach, who ruled over the monastery between the years 831 and 854, appears to have taken the *Mionna* of St. Columba back to Ireland in 849. All that is known of him is that his surname was Ua Finachta, and that he was slain by the Saxons in the year 854, when on a journey to Rome. The Annals of Ulster call him a co-arb of Columba.

Dunkeld and Abernethy

It is to this period that that great revolution belongs, which, as we have already said, led to the union of the kingdom of Dalriada and that of the Picts under the scepter of Kenneth MacAlpine. It appears to have been Kenneth's desire to reintroduce the Scottish clergy into his dominions and to restore them to the position which they had occupied in the preceding century. He even attempted to reclaim the monasteries in Lothian which had been originally Scottish foundations, and with this object made frequent incursions into that district, where he burned the monasteries of Dunbar and Melrose. Another important step toward the reestablishment of the Columban Church was the elevation of the church of Dunkeld to the position of primatial see. Here, probably as being the nearest Pictish church to Dalriada, and therefore a central position for the whole kingdom, Kenneth built a church, and removed to it part of the relics of St. Columba. This was in 850, the year following that in which Abbot Innrechtach had taken the *Mionna* back to Ireland. The primacy of the Columban monasteries in Ireland had, as we have seen, been already transferred to Kells, in Meath. By taking a part of St. Columba's relics to Dunkeld, Kenneth raised the latter place to the position of mother-church of his newly established kingdom, a step, no doubt, not without political advantages. The possession of the relics in question gave to the abbot of the newly founded monastery of Dunkeld a primacy over the Columban houses in Scotland, similar to that formerly enjoyed by Iona. Accordingly, in the year 865, the Annals of Ulster record the death of Tuathal MacArtguso, Abbot of Dunkeld and first Bishop of Fortrenn. The kingdom of the southern Picts was at this time known as Fortrenn, and Tuathal, as its bishop, was the acknowledged head of the Pictish Church.

During the reign of King Constantine, who succeeded his uncle Donald in 863, the primatial see appears to have been translated to Abernethy. The chronicles contain no direct record of such a translation; but various expressions contained in them seem to warrant the conclusion that it took place at this period. Bower, Abbot of Inchcolm, tells us in his *Scotichronicon* (written in the fourteenth century): "In the church of Abernethy there had been three elections of bishops when there was but one sole bishop in Scotland; and it was then the principal royal and pontifical seat, for some time, of the whole kingdom of the Picts." Historians of note have considered that Bower, whose statements have generally to be received with caution, is here reporting an authentic tradition. As regards the time when the three elections above mentioned were held, it cannot have been prior to the appointment of the Abbot of Dunkeld as first Bishop of Fortrenn, nor, on the other hand, subsequent to the transference of the primatial see to St. Andrews in the year 908. It must therefore have been between the death of Tuathal, first Bishop of the Picts, in 865, and the first appearance of the Bishop of St. Andrews in that position. "We have no record," observes Skene, "of the three bishops elected at Abernethy during this interval; but we may possibly find the name of one of them in the dedication of a neighboring parish. The church of Lathrisk, now Kettle, was dedicated to St. Ethernascus, whose day in the Scottish Calendar is December 22; and we find on the same day in the Irish Calendar Saints Ultan, Tua, and Iotharmaisc, at Claonadh (Clane), in the county of Kildare."

Norwegians on the west coast

Toward the middle of the ninth century, the Western Isles, as well as part of the mainland of west coast Scotland, had been occupied by the Norwegian Vikings; and the whole west coast, from Caithness to the Clyde, was now in their possession. It was in consequence, no doubt, of the danger to which Iona was exposed from these new enemies that the relics of St. Columba (including not only the Mionna but also the shrine containing his remains) were removed in 878 to Ireland. In the year 880 is recorded the death of Feradach, Abbot of Iona. He was succeeded by the last abbot of the line of Conall Gulban, the tribe of the patron saint, in the person of Flann, son of Maelduin, who died in 891. In 888 one of the same tribe, Maelbrigde, son of Tornan, had been elected Abbot of Armagh. He is styled "co-arb of Patrick and of Columcille," and Iona as well as Armagh appears to have become subject to him on the death of Flann, and to have thus lost its independent position. From the Life of St. Cadroe, however, a work written in the eleventh century, we learn that the shrine of St. Columba was afterward restored to Iona.

The Scottish Church

It is in the latter part of the ninth century that we first find definite mention of the "Scottish Church." Of King Cyric, or Grig, who reigned from 878 to 889, it is recorded that "he first gave liberty to the Scottish Church, which had been under servitude until now, according to the law and custom of the Picts." After the expulsion of the Columban monks from the Pictish territories at the commencement of the preceding century, the position of the Church was no doubt one of almost complete dependence on the secular power. King Grig, by restoring its ancient liberties, earned the gratitude of the clergy, who would not be likely to call in question the lawful title of a monarch from whom they had received such signal benefits. The question naturally arises, What is meant by the Church having been under servitude in former reigns? The reference is undoubtedly to the deprival of the immunities and exemptions usually attached to ecclesiastical property. One result of the expulsion of the Columban monks from the Pictish territory, at the beginning of the eighth century, had been that Church lands became subject to the same burdens and exactions that were laid upon other lands. These burdens were levied throughout the Pictish kingdom by the monarch, the *mormaers*, and *toiseachs*. King Grig no doubt issued a decree similar to the one enacted later by the Synod of Cashel, providing "that all Church lands and possessions be wholly free from exaction on the part of all secular persons, and that neither kings nor magnates are to exact, or to extort by force, victuals and hospitality in lands belonging to the Church."

The concessions thus granted by King Grig to the Church do not seem to have been of much advantage to the monarch himself. He was shortly afterward, with his pupil the son of Kenneth's daughter, driven out, and the crown, according to the Celtic custom, fell to his male descendants. These were now called kings of Alban, instead of, as heretofore, kings of the Picts; and the name of Alban was given to the whole country lying between the Forth and the Spey. The reign of the second of these kings of Alban was signalized by an event of importance to the Scottish Church. This was the great assembly held in the year 908 at the Moot-hill of Scone, at which King Constantine and Bishop Cellach of St. Andrews "solemnly vowed to protect the laws and discipline of the faith, and the rights of the churches and of the Gospel." Such an enactment was doubtless considered necessary owing to the repeated violations of ecclesiastical privilege which had taken place since the departure of King Grig. The prominent part taken by Bishop Cellach in this assembly points to the obvious conclusion that St. Andrews, and not Abernethy, had now become the seat of the primacy. Two lists of the bishops of St. Andrews have come down to us—one given by Bower of Inchcolm in his *Scotichronicon*, the other by Wyntoun, Prior of Lochleven. In both of these Cellach is called the first Bishop of St. Andrews. The assembly at Scone ratified the then organization of the Scottish Church under the Bishop of St. Andrews, who was known as "*Epscop Alban*" or Bishop of Alban.

Authorities differ as to the precise character of the assembly at Scone. According to Innes and Wilkins, it was a provincial council, while Hailes supposes that it was convened to establish and promulgate a national confession of faith. It is interesting to note that, like ecclesiastical councils in other parts of Christendom, the assembly was of a mixed nature—composed, that is, of secular as well as clerical dignitaries. The conjecture of Hailes, however, obviously belongs rather to the time of the Reformation than to the tenth century, at which period the formal publication of national confessions of faith was certainly not customary.

King Constantine deserves to hold a high place among the monarchs of Scotland. His constant endeavor during his long reign was to promote the welfare of the Church and the continued independence of his kingdom. In the evening of life he sought repose in the cloister. Entering the Culdee monastery of St. Andrews, he died there, full of years, in 953. St. Berchan touchingly describes his end: "Afterward God did call him to the monastery on the brink of the waves. In the House of the Apostle he came to death: undefiled was the pilgrim."

Constantine was succeeded, in the year 944, by Malcolm I, son of Donald II, and grandson of Kenneth MacAlpine. The most important event of his reign was the making over of the district of Cumberland to the Scottish crown, in 945, by Edmund of England. The condition of the grant was that Malcolm should be the faithful ally of the English king by land and sea. This act was transformed by later English chroniclers into a regular feudal transaction. The circumstances of the grant, however, are involved in great obscurity, and there is, besides, no trace of feudal fiefs in Scotland before the eleventh century.

Malcolm died in 953, and was followed, in accordance with the law of alternate succession, in turn by Indulf, son of Constantine, and by Duff, his own son, who reigned from 962 to 967. Fothad had meanwhile succeeded Cellach in the see of St. Andrews. The Chartulary of St. Andrews records the grant of the island of Lochleven by the *Keledei* of that place, and their Abbot Ronan, to Fothad, on condition of his undertaking to provide them with the necessaries of life. This was not a transfer with full rights of possession, but a conveyance by *precaria*, for purposes of protection and defence, such as were frequently made in the Middle Ages. Fordun mentions that Fothad was expelled from his see in 954 by King Indulf, and he also speaks of a celebrated copy of the Gospels, encased in silver, which he had himself seen, and which had belonged to Fothad, "the chief bishop of the Scots."

The Scottish Church in the late tenth century

Iona had now for a considerable period, in consequence of the occupation of the Western Isles by the Norwegians, been practically cut off from all connection with Scotland; and the abbacy had become to a great extent dependent on one of the Irish monasteries. We find, in 927, Dubthach, son of Duban, Abbot of Raphoe, who was of the race of Conall Gulban, becoming co-arb of St. Columba, in succession to Maelbrigde, Abbot of Armagh. The Ulster Annals record his death in the year 938, and the Four Masters style him "co-arb of Columcille and Adamnan, both in Erin and Alban."

The see of St. Andrews, vacant by the expulsion of Bishop Fothad, was held from 954 to 963 by Malisius, a disciple of St. Duthacus, or Dubhthach, mentioned above. During this period many pilgrims appear to have resorted to St. Andrews from Ireland. After the death of King Indulf, in 962, Fothad seems to have been restored to his see by King Duff, for the Four Masters record his death in 963, under the title of "Folhadh, son of Bran, scribe and Bishop of Inis Alban."

We have a prominent instance, about this time, of lay usurpation of ecclesiastical property in the abbacy of Dunkeld, held by a chieftain named Dunchad, or Duncan, who took part in the wars between Kings Duff and Colin, and was slain at the battle of Duncrub. The spiritual superintendence of the monastery remained in the hands of the prior.

Only very fragmentary notices have come down to us respecting the state of the Scottish Church from 967 to 976. The chronicles mention that Marcan, son of Breodolaig, was murdered in the church of St. Michael, that Leot and Slugadach went to Rome, Bishop Maelbrigde died, and Cellach, son of Ferdalaig, succeeded him. The cause of the journey to Rome here recorded is not given. The fact of its taking place immediately after a murder committed in one of the principal churches of the country naturally leads to the conjecture that Leot and Sluagadach were the culprits, and that their journey to the tomb of the apostles was to obtain absolution for their crime. Bower, however, in speaking of Cellach, states that he was the first bishop that went to Rome for confirmation. It is possible, therefore, that the cause of the journey to Rome was a dispute between two rival candidates for the bishopric, one of whom, perhaps, was slain in the sanctuary, while Cellach, the other, in order to disarm his opponents, appealed to the authority of the Pope, and sought his confirmation. Cellach held the see of St. Andrews from 970 to 995, during the reign of Kenneth II— a reign important to the Scottish Church, inasmuch as it witnessed the foundation of the church of Brechin, dedicated to the Holy Trinity. The short notice of this event in the Chronicle runs thus: "He it is [Kenneth] who gave the great city of Brechin to the Lord." It is only from later history that we learn that the monastery erected there was built after the Irish model, in proof of which, indeed, we have the ancient round tower, which still remains. "The churches," says Skene, "which afterward formed the diocese of Brechin, were probably, even at this early period, possessions of the new foundation at Brechin. In the districts of Angus and Mearns the churches were shared between the dioceses of Brechin and St.

Andrews, in a manner so irregular and unsystematic as to point to a mixed population of Picts and Scots. It seems to have been through the medium of the recovery of the old foundations, and the creation of new, that a Scottish population was spread over the country; and the object of King Kenneth in this foundation may have been to bring a Pictish population more under the direct influence of the Scots. The church of Brechin was founded during the time that Mughron was co-arb of Columcille both in Erin and Alban, when probably there was freer intercourse between the Scottish and Irish Churches."

Iona again ravaged by Danes

The period following the death of Mughron, which took place when he had held the co-arbship for sixteen years, was a very disastrous one for Iona. Danes and Norwegians were at this time struggling for the possession of the Western Isles, where the latter had been settled for a considerable period. The Danes on their side, by the acquisition of the Isle of Man, had obtained an important position for the carrying on of naval warfare. Florence of Worcester calls Maccus, son of Aralt, their chief, "king of many islands," but it is uncertain how far his sway extended. The Danes far exceeded the Norwegians in cruelty and ferocity. In the last year of Mughron's life, Anlaf Cuaron, King of the Danes at Dublin, came on a pilgrimage to Iona, where he lived the life of a penitent and afterward died. This monarch was son-in-law to King Constantine of Scotland, and had been baptized when ruling over the Danes of Northumbria. The successor of Mughron, however, Maelciarain ua Maigne, was slain by the Danes at Dublin, or, as the chronicle has it, "suffered red martyrdom from the Danes." This was in 986; and on Christmas Eve of the same year, Iona was plundered and the abbot slaughtered, with fifteen of his monks. A few months later the Danes were attacked in force by Sigurd, Earl of Orkney, who defeated them with great slaughter. Gofraigh, their king, was killed in Dalriada, and the Norwegians resumed their sway over the Western Isles. A spot is still pointed out in Iona, known as the "White Bay of the Monks," as the place where the abbot and his brethren met their death. This was the last attack upon Iona by the Danes, who, not long after, were converted to Christianity.

With regard to the relics of St. Columba, the following is the tradition reported by Colman, on the authority of St. Berchan. Manderus, son of the King of Denmark, and leader of a fleet of Northmen, came, in the course of his ravages through North Britain, to Iona, where these servants of Satan, mixing sacred things with profane, excavated the ground in search of hidden treasure. Among others, they found the sarcophagus in which was a precious treasure—namely, the body of St. Columba. This they took on board their ship, and on their voyage to Ireland they opened it; but finding nothing therein but bones and ashes, shut it again, and threw it into the sea. The waves cast it ashore at Downpatrick, in Ireland, and the abbot of that place, learning in a vision what were its contents, placed it along with the relics of St. Patrick and St. Bridget. In the following century the shrine was certainly believed to be at Downpatrick, or Dun. "In Dun," says the old tract known as the *Amra Columcille*, "the resurrection of Columcille will be, as the poet has said—

> Iona with the multitude of its relics,
> Of which was Colum, beauteous disciple;
> He went out yet at last,
> So that Dun is his blessed church."

In the reign of Kenneth II (970–994), a new province was added to the Scottish kingdom by the cession of the district of Lothian to Kenneth by Edgar, King of England. By thus relinquishing his claim to a territory which, owing to the Danish settlements in Northumbria, it was difficult for him to hold securely, Edgar gained the faithful alliance of the Scots against their common enemy, the Danes. In addition to Cumberland, which had been united to Scotland under Malcolm I, Kenneth also acquired possession of the district of Cumbria, lying between the Clyde and the Solway Firth. The last prince of this territory was Dumeaill, or Donald, who is recorded to have gone on a pilgrimage to Rome, where he died. Together with the territory of Cumbria, Galloway was also incorporated into the Scottish kingdom. The disintegration of the kingdom of Northumbria had resulted in the quasi-independence of the various nationalities which had been included in it; and it was long before their final settlement and absorption into one or other of the northern and southern kingdoms. King Kenneth, according to the Annals of Ulster, was slain in 995, by Fenella, daughter of the Earl of Angus.

St. Cadroe

One of the few Scottish saints of this period of whom we have any authentic knowledge is St. Cadroe, who was nearly related to the royal house of Scotland. He received his training in the famous school of Armagh, and on his return to Scotland sought out youths of talent and promise, whom he educated for the priesthood. The esteem in which he was held by King Constantine is shown by the fact of that monarch accompanying him on his departure from Scotland, as far as the borders of Northumbria. Cadroe betook himself to Odo, Archbishop of Canterbury, and thence to France, where he entered the Benedictine Order at Fleury-sur-Loire, and subsequently became abbot of the monastery of Walciodorus. He is buried at Metz.

Malcolm II

In the year 1005 Malcolm II ascended the Scottish throne, which he occupied for close upon thirty years. A century and a half had now elapsed since the royal race of Scottish Dalriada had first obtained possession of the Pictish crown. The title of "Kings of the Picts," which they had borne for the first fifty years, had given place to that of "Kings of Alban," and the Pictish and Scottish populations had gradually become to a great extent amalgamated. The process of consolidation advanced rapidly during the long reign of Malcolm, and it was now that the kingdom first became known as Scotia, from the dominant race to which its inhabitants belonged.

Not long before Malcolm's accession, Sigurd, Earl of Orkney, had been converted to Christianity under the influence of Olav Tryggvesson, the first Christian king of Norway. Olav was returning to Norway, in the year 997, from an expedition to the Hebrides, when he came upon Sigurd, who was lying with a single ship under the Isle of Hoy, and took him prisoner. Olav offered him freedom on condition of his embracing Christianity, acknowledging the sovereignty of Norway, and proclaiming the Christian faith in the Orkneys. Hundi, the son of Sigurd, went with Olav as a hostage to Norway, where he died after some years. Sigurd himself fell at the great battle fought at Clontarf, near Dublin, in 1014, between the allied Danish and Norwegian forces and the native tribes of Ireland, led by the renowned Brian Boroimhe. The death of Sigurd was fatal to Norwegian power in Scotland. Such of their possessions as had not been completely colonized by them, and were thus only partially connected with Norway, passed at once into the possession of the Scottish crown. Such was the case with the province of Caithness, which was claimed by King Malcolm as a dependency of the Scottish kingdom, and by him granted as an earldom to his grandson Thorfinn. Other provinces, such as Moray and Ross, had been in still slighter connection with Norway, to whom they had merely paid an annual tribute, while they still retained their hereditary chiefs or princes. These provinces became, at Sigurd's death, completely independent of Norway.

After the great victory gained against the Northumbrians at Carham, in 1018, Malcolm is recorded "to have distributed many oblations to the churches as well as to the clergy." The account given by Fordun of the foundation of the church of Mortlach, situated in the north-east of Scotland between the Dee and the Spey, is not found in the old chronicles, and is probably based on some confusion on the part of Fordun between Malcolm II and Malcolm III, and between the foundation of the bishopric of Aberdeen with that of Mortlach. The result of the battle of Carham was the cession to King Malcolm, by Eadwulf Cudel, Earl of Northumbria, of the whole district north of the Tweed, which thus became the southern boundary of Scotland. Malcolm appears to have restored to the Abbot of Iona the title of co-arb of Columcille. In 1007 Abbot Muredach is recorded to have resigned the co-arbship, in order to become a recluse, and to have been succeeded by Ferdomnach, "with the advice of the men of Erin."

From 1025 to 1028 the see of St. Andrews was held by Alwyn. It was about this period that Malcolm gave his eldest daughter in marriage to Crinan, lay Abbot of Dunkeld. From this union descended a dynasty of kings which was destined to extinguish that ancient church, with its peculiar institutions, whence they themselves had originally sprung. The steps by which Dunkeld had come to be a lay possession are easily traced. We have seen the original Culdee church, founded by Constantine, become the seat of a Scottish monastery and of the Bishop of Fortrenn, or Primate of Scotland. Then, when the bishopric was transferred to Abernethy, the successor of the abbot-bishop appears simply as "*princeps*," which might apply to a layman as well as to a cleric. Abbot Duncan, who fell at the battle of Duncrub, was evidently a layman. Finally, we have Crinan, Abbot of Dunkeld, marrying one of the daughters of the king. Besides the large possessions of Dunkeld, lying in the very center of the kingdom, Crinan also held the property of the monastery of Dull, in the districts of Atholl and Argyll. Crinan fell fighting against the Norwegians in the year 1045. The lands belonging to Dunkeld remained with his descendants, but the buildings of the abbey had been some years previously entirely destroyed by fire.

Family inheritance of Church property

Not only in Scotland, but in Ireland also, the canker which was at this time eating into the Church was the concubinage of the clergy, with its natural result, the system of hereditary succession to benefices. In proportion to the strictness with which celibacy had been observed during the monastic period of the Church was the laxness on this point which prevailed among the secular clergy of the period which succeeded. From the widespread transgression of the law of celibacy naturally followed the introduction of a hereditary succession to benefices among the families of the clergy. The secularization of Church property was further promoted by the fact of the abbots and other ecclesiastics not taking orders, but performing their clerical functions by means of vicars, or of the *Cele De*, if such happened to be attached to the Church. Usurpation of the abbeys and benefices by great secular chieftains, and the so-called marriage of the clergy, were the two principal means by which the property of the Church was taken from her and transferred to in laymen. We have the testimony of Giraldus Cambrensis, speaking of the church of Llanpadarn Vawr, to the prevalence of this abuse in Wales. And the great St. Bernard, in his Life of St. Malachy of Armagh, speaks in very severe terms of the state of the Irish Church at the beginning of the twelfth century. "A most evil custom," he says, "had sprung up through the ambition of certain nobles, that the holy see should be obtained by hereditary succession. For they suffered none to be made bishops except they were of their own tribe and family. Nor was it for a short time only that this execrable succession continued, since fifteen generations had already passed away in this evil practice. And so firmly had this wicked and adulterous generation established their impious right, or rather wrong, worthy of death, that even if clergy of their family were sometimes wanting to them, yet bishops never were. Hence arose in Ireland that universal laxness of discipline whereof we have already spoken, that weakening of restraint and decay of religion: hence came about the prevalence of barbarous cruelty instead of Christian mildness, and the introduction of a kind of paganism under the nominal form of Christianity."

Numerous instances of hereditary succession, in abbacies as well as in other offices, are recorded in the Irish annals from the ninth to the eleventh century. Ecclesiastical property was handed down in families as a matter of course. In Scotland the extensive territories attached to the great monasteries were known as the *Abdaine* or abbacy, and this was generally in the hands of secular nobles. Thus we find Crinan, lay Abbot of Dunkeld, in possession of the Abdaine of Dull, which included the whole of the present parishes of Dull and Fortingall.

Duncan and Macbeth

King Malcolm II died in 1034, and with him the male line of Kenneth MacAlpine became extinct. Had there been any male descendant in existence, the integrity of the kingdom would have been in danger; for he would have had a claim, by the ancient law of succession, as tracing his descent to the founder of the line, to the kingdom of Alban proper, while the more recently acquired territories of Cumbria and Lothian would have passed to Malcolm's heirs in the female line. No male scion of the race, however, was now living, for the last had been slain by Malcolm himself a year before his death, perhaps with the object of making way for the peaceable accession of his grandson Duncan to the entire kingdom. At all events Duncan, who was son of Abbot Crinan of Dunkeld and of Malcolm's eldest daughter, succeeded to the crown in 1034 without opposition. A few years later, however, Eadulf, Earl of Northumbria, invaded and laid waste the whole of Cumbria. Duncan, on his side, advanced against Durham with a powerful force, but all his efforts to carry that stronghold proved unavailing. In the north, Duncan found himself in conflict with his cousin Thorfinn, who, on coming into possession of the entire earldom of Orkney, refused to give up Caithness to the king, on the ground that it had been granted to him by his grandfather Malcolm. The Sagas relate that a great battle was fought in Moray in which the king was worsted.

Duncan was slain on the 14th of August 1040 by his general, Macbeth, who succeeded him in the kingdom and reigned for seventeen years. Macbeth was connected with the family of his predecessor through his wife Gruoch, the daughter of that Bode whose son or grandson had been put to death by Malcolm, with the probable object, as we have seen, of securing Duncan's succession. There seemed thus to be a sort of nemesis in Macbeth's obtaining the crown. His claim does not appear to have been disputed by the Scots, and his reign was on the whole a prosperous one. Of his goodwill toward the Church we are not without record. We find him granting the lands of Kyrkness and Bolgyne to the Culdees of Lochleven, "for the benefit of their prayers," and "with the highest veneration and devotion."

An attempt made in the year 1045 by Crinan, Abbot of Dunkeld, to drive Macbeth from the throne, resulted in the complete defeat of the opposing party and in the death of Crinan himself. About 1050 Macbeth appears to have gone to Rome, probably to obtain absolution for the murder of Duncan. Marianus Scotus has left on record his munificence to the Roman poor. The next few years were devoted by Macbeth to establishing and consolidating his usurped throne. The fact of Duncan's sons being still in infancy, together with the powerful support of the Earl of Orkney, were no doubt of great advantage to his position. Nevertheless, the hour of his fall was approaching. Siward, Earl of Northumbria, who was doubly related to Crinan of Dunkeld, determined to avenge Duncan's death. Siward's sister or cousin had married Duncan, and had had by him a son Malcolm, who on the overthrow of Macbeth ascended the throne as Malcolm III. For three years longer Macbeth succeeded in holding the kingdom, but he was finally driven across the Grampians, and slain by Malcolm in Marr on the 15th of August 1057.

During the reigns of Duncan and Macbeth the see of St. Andrews was filled by Maelduin, said by Bower to be the son of Gillandris. The Chronicles call him Maldunus, and record his liberality to the Culdees of Lochleven, to whom he gave the church of Markinch with all its land. Tighernach tells us that, in 1055, Maelduin, Bishop of Alban, who gave orders to the clergy of the Gaels, died in Christ; and Wyntoun mentions that he had held the bishopric for twenty-seven years. Maelduin was succeeded by Tuthald, who occupied the see for only four years, during which time he also granted a church (that of Scoonie) to the Culdees. It was during the long tenure of the bishopric by Fothad, the successor of Tuthald, that the Norman conquest of England took place—an event pregnant with issues of the deepest moment to the Scottish Church, inasmuch as one of its results was the close of the monastic period of her history, and the introduction and development of the normal system of diocesan government.

CHAPTER 8

ST. MARGARET,
QUEEN OF SCOTLAND

St. Margaret, whose union with the Scottish king was destined to exercise so important and beneficent an influence, not only on the characters of her husband and children, but on the Scottish Church at large, was the great-niece of Edward the Confessor, and grand-daughter of Edmund Ironsides, who fell by the dagger of Ardric in 1017. Canute, King of England, undertook the guardianship of Edmund's two sons, Edward and Edmund, whom he sent to be educated at the Swedish Court, with the object of estranging them as far as possible from England, and thus consolidating his own power in the kingdom. From Sweden they came to Hungary, where Edward married the Princess Agatha, sister to the King of Hungary. From this union sprang a son, Edgar, surnamed Atheling, and two daughters, Margaret and Christina. In the year 1041, on the death of Harold, who five years before had succeeded Canute on the throne of England, Edward the Confessor became king, and his nephew Edward returned, with his children, to his native country. In 1066 was fought the great battle of Hastings, in which the Saxons were vanquished by their Norman invaders; and shortly afterward Edgar Atheling, the heir of the Saxon royal house, fled to Scotland. His mother, Agatha, and his sisters, Margaret and Christina, accompanied him, and the royal fugitives were hospitably welcomed by Malcolm III to his kingdom.

A marriage was soon afterwards arranged between Margaret and the Scottish king, whose first wife Ingibiorge, a princess of Norway, appears to have died soon after giving birth to a son, named Duncan. The marriage was solemnized in the spring of the year 1069, probably at Dunfermline, by Fothad, Bishop of St. Andrews. Dunfermline was now the principal seat of the Scottish kings, for which it was well adapted, from the natural strength of its position; and we read that Malcolm and his queen founded a church there in honor of the Blessed Trinity, on the occasion of their marriage.

In depicting the life of St. Margaret, the historian is fortunate in finding himself able to make use of a biography of the holy queen compiled by one of her contemporaries. Turgot, Margaret's confessor, Prior of Durham, and subsequently Bishop of St. Andrews, has faithfully recorded the chief events of a life wholly dedicated to the service of God and the welfare of the Scottish people. For many years he was a constant witness of the heroic love of God and her neighbor in which Margaret's life was spent, and that life could therefore find no fitter biographer than himself. There is an air of simple veracity about his narrative which commends it to the reader as the work of an eminent lover of truth, and it throws considerable light not only on the history of Margaret and the members of her family, but on the state of the Scottish Church and kingdom at the momentous epoch of the Norman conquest of England.

"There is perhaps," observes Skene, "no more beautiful character recorded in history than that of Margaret. For purity of motives, for an earnest desire to benefit the people among whom her lot was cast, for a deep sense of religion and great personal piety, for the unselfish performance of whatever duty lay before her, and for entire self-abnegation, she is unsurpassed, and the chroniclers of the time all bear witness to her exalted character." "This distinguished princess," Ordericus Vitalis says of her, "descended from a long line of kings, was still more eminent for her great worth and the sanctity of her life." The mortifications practiced by the holy queen, especially in the matter of fasting and abstinence, which far exceeded what was commanded by the law of the Church, brought upon her an infirmity which lasted her whole life. In works of charity of every kind she was indefatigable. Besides the daily alms which were regularly distributed in the palace, she embraced every opportunity of succoring the poor and distressed. The king was accustomed to offer coins of gold in the church at High Mass; and these, Turgot tells us, the queen would "devoutly pillage," and bestow them on the beggars who sought her help.

The influence which St. Margaret exercised on her royal husband is described by Turgot in glowing terms. "I confess," he says, "I was astonished at the great miracle of God's mercy, when I perceived in the king such a steady earnestness in his devotion, and I wondered how it was that there could exist in the heart of a man living in the world such an entire sorrow for sin." King and queen alike, in all that they did, aimed only at the glory of God and the fulfillment of His divine will. And the wonderful harmony which knit their souls together found, as was natural, its reflection in their external lives, which one spirit seemed to rule and animate. Perfect order and discipline reigned in the royal household. The queen and the ladies of her Court were constantly employed in making vestments and other ornaments for the divine service, and her attendants were taught frequently to exercise themselves in works of piety and charity. All alike regarded their saintly mistress with equal love and veneration, and not so much as the least unseemly word was ever uttered in her presence. Her care St. Margaret was no less admirable and exemplary in her relation of mother than in that of wife. In her constant solicitude for the welfare of her people, she did not forget her obligations toward her own family. The care of their education she regarded as one of her highest duties, and herself instructed them in the principles of true religion. "O my children," she would often say to them, "fear the Lord; for they that fear Him shall lack nothing. Love Him, for His love will never fail you, and will give you prosperity in this life, and everlasting happiness with all the saints." Night and day did this Christian mother offer up her prayers to God for her children. Amid the pressure of her public and domestic duties, she yet found time, her biographer tells us, to devote herself with wonderful assiduity to the Word of God. She possessed not only a remarkable intellect, but also a wonderful gift of eloquent speaking; and such a deep knowledge of religion did she acquire through her profound study of the Holy Scriptures, that even learned doctors often left her presence far wiser men than when they entered it. Lanfranc, Archbishop of Canterbury, had been her instructor in the spiritual life; and that saintly prelate, in a letter to his royal pupil, cannot find words to express the high esteem in which he holds her.

It was not long before Margaret directed her attention to the state of the Scottish Church, and to the work of bringing about a reform of certain abuses connected with it. She found prevailing in the ancient Church of her adopted country a number of customs which were at variance with the practice of the universal Church, and which, as it appeared to her, had no just claim to longer toleration. At the instance of the queen several councils were held in reference to the matter in question; and at the principal of these councils, Turgot tells us, "she, with a very few of her friends, combated the defenders of a perverse custom with the sword of the Spirit, that is, the Word of God; while her husband, who knew the English language quite as well as his own, was a most careful interpreter for either side."

The first subject under discussion was the manner peculiar to the Celts of observing the forty days' fast of Lent. The queen, after first dwelling on the necessity of a due harmony between faith and practice, proceeded to point out that the universal Church commenced the forty days' fast on Ash Wednesday, while the Celts were in the habit of beginning it on the Monday of the following week. To the argument brought forward by the other side, that they acted on the authority of the Gospels, according to which Christ fasted for six weeks, Margaret rejoined that our Lord is related to have fasted for forty days, whereas the Celtic practice, by reason of the six Sundays being deducted, was to fast only on thirty-six. The duty was therefore incumbent on them of adding four days to their fast, in order to be at one with the observance of the Holy Church throughout the world. The argument was effectual; and "convinced," says Turgot, "by this plain demonstration of the truth, they began henceforth the solemnities of the fasts as Holy Church does everywhere." The fast of forty days observed by our Lord was no doubt a continuous one, not excluding the Sabbath days: and this appears to have been the ground of the Celtic practice. From the earliest times, however, the Church has never allowed Sundays to be observed as fasting days; and centuries before the time of St. Margaret it had been the almost universal practice to begin the fast of Lent upon Ash Wednesday, in order to make up the full number of forty days.

In the second place, the queen inquired of the Celtic ecclesiastics how they justified their practice of "not receiving on the festival of Easter the Sacrament of the Body and Blood of Christ, according to the usage of the Holy and Apostolic Church." They answered her thus: "The Apostle teaches that those who eat and drink unworthily eat and drink judgment to themselves; and since we acknowledge ourselves to be sinners, we fear to approach that mystery, lest we should eat and drink judgment to ourselves." "What then?" was Margaret's answer, "shall no one that is a sinner taste of that holy mystery? If so, no one whatever dare approach it, for no one is sinless—not even the infant that has lived but one day upon the earth. And if no one may partake of it, wherefore does Christ proclaim in His Gospel, 'Except you shall eat the flesh of the Son of Man and drink His blood, you shall not have life in you?' But the saying of the apostle which you quote is, according to the interpretation of the fathers, to be otherwise understood. He does not hold all sinners to be unworthy of the sacrament of salvation; for after saying, 'He eats and drinks judgment to himself,' he adds, 'not discerning the Lords body'—that is, not distinguishing it by faith from corporal food. It is the man who partakes of the holy mysteries carrying with him the defilements of his sins, without confession or penance, that eats and drinks judgment to himself. But we who many days before have confessed our sins, have cleansed our souls by penance, and washed away our stains by alms-giving and many tears, and then on Easter Day draw near in Catholic faith to the table of the Lord and receive the body of the Lamb without spot—we eat and drink not to judgment but to the remission of our sins." Again the arguments of the queen prevailed: "Knowing now," says Turgot, "the meaning of the Church's practices, they observed them ever after in the sacrament of salvation."

A third point which Margaret was desirous of enforcing was the abolition of certain "barbarous rites "in which masses were wont to be celebrated in some parts of Scotland. What these barbarous rites were we are not told, but the allusion is not improbably to the use of the native language in the celebration of Mass instead of Latin.

The queen further protested against the prevailing abuse of Sunday desecration. "Let us," she said, "venerate the Lord's Day, inasmuch as upon it our Savior rose from the dead: let us do no servile work on that day, whereon we were redeemed from the

slavery of the devil." So powerfully did these and similar arguments weigh with the Scots, and with such strictness, in consequence, did they observe in future the sanctity of the Sunday,
that no one, we are told, dared on that day to carry any burdens
himself or to compel others to do so. The Scots in this matter had
no doubt kept up the traditional practice of the ancient monastic
Church of Ireland, which observed Saturday rather than Sunday
as the day of rest. Adamnan has told us how St. Columba, on the
last Saturday of his life, said to his faithful attendant Diarmaid:
"This day in the Holy Scriptures is called the Sabbath, which
means rest: and it is indeed a Sabbath to me, for it is the last day
of my present laborious life, and on it I rest after the fatigues of
my labors. This night at midnight, which commences the solemn
Lord's Day, I shall go the way of our fathers." The Celtic Church,
as has already been pointed out, while observing the Lord's Day
as a religious solemnity, appears to have followed the Jews in
resting from labor on the Saturday.

The last abuse touched upon by the queen was forbidden
that of marriages within the forbidden degrees. So far had this
been carried by the Scots, that the impediment of affinity even
in the first degree, and lineally as well as collaterally, was entirely
disregarded by them; so that for a man to marry his deceased
brother's wife, or even his stepmother, was far from unusual.
This unnatural custom was not confined to Scotland: Giraldus
Cambrensis makes it a matter of accusation against the Irish in
the ninth century; and Pope Alexander III afterward denounced
the same practice in still stronger language.

Turgot tells us that Margaret succeeded in condemning and
expelling from her realm many other inveterate abuses. He
makes, however, no explicit mention of two of the most prominent of these, which were, moreover, connected most intimately
with ecclesiastical discipline, and had long been fruitful sources
of manifold evil both to Church and State. The council, as far as

we know, did not touch upon the question of the lay usurpation of ecclesiastical property, or on the widespread abuse of clerical concubinage. It may have been the thought of her husband and her son that prevented Margaret from dwelling on these points. "Possibly," says Skene, "she was restrained by the knowledge that the royal house into which she had married owed its origin to the lay abbots of one of the principal monasteries, and was largely endowed with the possessions of the Church; and if in the council her eye lighted upon her young son Ethelred, who, even in boyhood, was lay Abbot of Dunkeld, her utterances on the subject could hardly be otherwise than checked."

As might have been expected, the monastic institutions of the country found in the holy queen a warm friend and protector, and we are told that she showed special favor to the anchorites who dwelt at that period in various parts of Scotland. Turgot's narrative has here a particular interest, not only for the insight which it gives us into the devotion and humility which characterized St. Margaret, but also as affording us a glimpse at the manner of life practiced by the anchorites. "There were at this period," he tells us, "in many places throughout the realm of Scotland persons shut up in different cells, and leading lives of great strictness; in the flesh, but not according to the flesh; for being upon earth, they led the life of angels. These the queen busied herself in often visiting and conversing with, for in them she loved and venerated Christ, and would recommend herself to their prayers. As she could not induce them to accept any earthly gift from her, she urgently entreated them to be so good as to bid her perform some alms-deed or work of mercy; and this devout woman did forthwith fulfill whatever was their pleasure, either by helping the poor out of their poverty, or by relieving the distressed in their troubles, whatever these might be. Since the church of St. Andrews was much frequented by the devout, who flocked to it from all quarters, she erected dwellings so that the pilgrims might shelter there and rest themselves after the fatigues of their journey. She had arranged that they should there find all they needed for the refreshment of the body. Servants were appointed, whose special duty it was to see that everything that might be required for these wayfarers should be always in readiness. Moreover, she provided ships for the transport of the pilgrims, nor was it lawful to demand any fee for the passage." Among the anchorites here alluded to were doubtless the Culdees of Lochleven, to whom, as we are told elsewhere, the king and queen "devoutly gave the town of Ballechristin," and who also received from Bishop Fothad—"a man of most pious memory, with whose life and doctrine the whole region of the Scots was happily enlightened"—a grant of the church of Auchterderran.

In the zeal and devotion displayed by Margaret in promoting the welfare of religion in Scotland, she was not likely to overlook the claims of the most venerable institutions of the country—the mother house of Iona, new fallen to ruins in the storms of war and the lapse of ages. "The faithful queen," we are told by Ordericus Vitalis, "rebuilt the monastery, granted it an endowment for the carrying on of the Lord's work, and restored the monks." What was rebuilt at this time appears to have been the monastery proper, which had probably been in ruins since the great Danish attack in 986: the church and oratory, whose remains belong to a much earlier period, were no doubt still entire. King Malcolm in 1093, a few months before his death, ceded the Western Isles to Magnus, King of Norway, who afterward came to Iona and visited the shrine of St. Columba. In the year 1099 died Dunchad, grandson of Moenaig, the last of the old abbots of Iona.

Malcolm perished on November 13, 1093, apparently by the treachery of one of his own followers, on the banks of the river Alne, in Northumberland, whither he had led an army in order to revenge the insults he had received from William Rufus, the haughty successor of the Conqueror on the English throne. He was buried at Tynemouth, whence his remains were afterward removed to Dunfermline by his son Alexander.

Queen Margaret did not long survive the loss of her husband. She was already dangerously ill when her son Edgar arrived from the Scottish army with the disastrous tidings of his father's death. Raising her eyes and hands to heaven, the holy queen gave thanks to God, saying, "I give You praise, Almighty God, for that You have been pleased that I should endure such deep sorrow at my departing; and I trust that by means of this suffering, it is Your pleasure that I should be cleansed from some of the stains of my sins." Fortified by the reception of the sacraments, she passed away calmly and peacefully on the 16th of November 1093, in the forty-seventh year of her age, and the twenty-second of her wedded life. She was buried in the Abbey of Dunfermline.

The universal belief in her sanctity which prevailed throughout Britain was solemnly sanctioned by Innocent IV, in 1250, on the 19th of June in which year her body was taken from the grave and placed under the high altar, in a silver shrine, adorned with precious stones. The Church commemorates her on the 16th of November, the day of her death.

CHAPTER 9

NEW FOUNDATIONS
IN SCOTLAND

Edgar

Malcolm's long reign of thirty-five years had been a period of such unwonted prosperity and peace that his death was a great misfortune for the country. The work of consolidating the various races under his rule had been greatly advanced, not only by his personal claims upon their allegiance, but by the civilizing influence of his virtuous and accomplished queen. The death of Malcolm raised once more the vexed question of succession to the throne, which had been in abeyance for more than thirty years, and the kingdom seemed to be in danger of dissolution. By his first wife, Ingibiorge, widow of Thorfinn, Earl of Orkney, Malcolm had two sons—Duncan, who had been delivered as a hostage to the King of England in 1072, and Donald, who predeceased him in 1085. By his second marriage, with Margaret, he had, besides two daughters, six sons: Edward, who fell with his father in Northumbria; Edmund; Ethelred, whom we have already seen as lay Abbot of Dunkeld; Edgar; Alexander; and David. The struggles of the various pretenders to the throne ended with the victory of Edgar, who reigned from 1097 to 1107.

One of Edgar's first acts, on finding himself firmly established on the throne, was the re-foundation of the monastery at Coldingham, which had been destroyed by the Danes. In his charter of foundation he sets forth that he had come to the dedication of the Church of St. Mary at Coldingham, which dedication had been carried out to the honor of God and to his contentment, and that he had offered on the altar the whole town of Swintun as a gift to the same church, to be held forever by the monks of St. Cuthbert. He further mentions that he had imposed upon the men of Coldinghamshire the annual payment of half a mark of silver to the monks for each plow. This last stipulation is noticeable as presenting to us for the first time something like a parochial district attached to a church; and we find in another charter still clearer mention of the establishment of a parish church. In this document Thor informs Earl David, his lord, that King Edgar had given him Ednaham (Ednam) in Berwickshire; that he had built there a church, which the king had dedicated to St. Cuthbert; that he had endowed it with one plow, and now prays for confirmation of the grant he had made to St. Cuthbert and the monks of Durham. Here, evidently, we have the formation of a manor with its parish church, which, in a subsequent document, is termed the mother church of Ednam.

Alexander

Edgar, who is described as a prince of singularly mild and peace-loving disposition, died in 1107; and the kingdom was thereupon divided between his two brothers, Alexander and David. To the former, who succeeded to the kingly title, was assigned the territory north of the Forth and the Clyde; while the district of Cumbria and the southern part of Lothian fell to David, with the title of comes or earl.

During the reign of Edgar no steps appear to have been taken toward filling up the see of St. Andrews, which had been vacant for several years. Alexander, however, immediately on his accession to the throne, set himself to the carrying out of the policy inaugurated by his mother, Margaret, that of reorganizing the Scottish Church on the English model, or, in other words, of substituting for the monastic system which had prevailed for centuries the normal form of diocesan and parochial organization. As a first step toward the accomplishment of this design, Alexander, in the first year of his reign, procured the appointment of Turgot, Prior of Durham, and formerly confessor to Queen Margaret, to the see of St. Andrews.

Besides taking steps to fill up the vacancy in the bishopric of St. Andrews, Alexander signalized the commencement of his reign by the creation of the two additional sees of Moray and Dunkeld. The country lying beyond the Spey was at this time, owing to Scandinavian influence, but slenderly connected with the Scottish kingdom, and only very scanty notices of the condition of the Church in these districts have come down to us. Doubtless, however, the favorable climate and fertile soil of the southern shores of the Moray Firth would recommend that locality as advantageous for ecclesiastical foundations. Hither in the eighth century St. Gervadius or Gernadius had come from his native Ireland to preach the Christian faith, and here he had founded the church of Keneder. A cave and a spring in the neighborhood of Elgin still bear his name. There do not appear to have been any traces of Culdee settlements in the district when Alexander founded the bishopric of Moray. Until the time of Bricius, the sixth bishop, who held the see from 1203 to 1233, there does not seem to have been any fixed episcopal residence, and the previous bishops had their seat in Birnie, Spynie, or Keneder. Bricius, who was present at the Fourth Lateran Council in Rome in 1215, fixed the see at Spynie, where he founded a chapter of eight canons. His successor, Andrew de Moravia, transferred it to Elgin, which continued to be the seat of the Bishops of Moray until the Reformation, and where arose a noble cathedral, consecrated by Gilbert, Bishop of Caithness, on July 15, 1224.

South-east of Moray was the second diocese founded by Alexander, that of Dunkeld. The church of Dunkeld had already for more than two centuries held a prominent place in the ecclesiastical organization of the country. It had been founded, as we have seen, or rather, restored, by Kenneth MacAlpine, who had constituted it the primatial see of his kingdom, and had removed thither part of the relics of St. Columba. Subsequently, together with the extensive territories granted to it by successive monarchs, it had fallen into the possession of lay abbots, from one of whom, Crinan, was sprung the royal house now on the throne of Scotland. It was in the year 1107 that King Alexander erected Dunkeld into a cathedral church, superseding the Culdees, and establishing in their place a bishop and chapter of secular canons. It is interesting to note the survival, in the new order of things, of the ancient primacy of Dunkeld over the Columban foundations in Scotland. Besides the great lay abbacies of Dull and Glendochart, comprising what was afterwards the diocese of Argyll, we find the new bishopric exercising rights over various churches in other dioceses, which represented old Columban foundations. In charters to the abbey of Dunfermline, the rights of Dunkeld in Fife and Fotherif are expressly reserved. In Fife the bishopric possessed the island of Inchcolm, dedicated to St. Columba, with adjacent parts of the mainland; and in Angus the districts of Fearn and Menmuir, dedicated to the Columban bishop St. Aidan.

Another important step taken by Alexander in the carrying out of his ecclesiastical policy was the introduction of religious orders and communities who would take the place of the Culdees and inspire new life into the Scottish Church. In the year 1115 a body of canons regular of St. Augustine, known as black canons, came to Scotland from the monastery of St. Oswald's, near Pontefract, at the invitation of King Alexander and his queen Sibilla (daughter of Henry I of England), who gave to them the church of Scone. On the death of Eadmer, in 1124, Robert, Prior of Scone, was nominated by the king to the bishopric of St. Andrews. A few years after the foundation of Scone, the canons regular were introduced into the diocese of Dunkeld. Alexander founded a priory for them in 1122, on an island in Loch Tay, where his queen Sibilla afterward died and was buried; and another, in the island of Inchcolm, in the Firth of Forth, the following year. This monastery, which is styled by Boece "a carbuncle among precious stones," was founded by the king in gratitude for hospitality he had received from a hermit living on the island, who had entertained him for three days in his cell. Walter Bower, the continuator of the Chronicle of Fordun, died here in 1449. One of Alexander's last acts was to confer upon the church of Scone the right to hold a court. He died at Stirling in April 1124, and was buried in the abbey of Dunfermline. Fordun describes him as a "lettered and godly man of large heart, zealous in building churches, open-handed to all comers, and devoted to the poor." Aelred also, in his *Genealogia Regum*, speaks highly of his character.

David I

Alexander, dying without issue, was succeeded on the throne by his brother David, the youngest son of Malcolm and Margaret. He had accompanied his sister Matilda, on her marriage with Henry I, to the English Court, where he received his education and was trained in the feudal usages of the time. In the year 1110 he married Matilda, widow of Simon de Senlis, Earl of Northampton. Scottish by descent, but an Englishman in education and habits, David was thoroughly penetrated by the feudal ideas which prevailed at the Anglo-Norman Court, and he was not long in giving expression to them on his accession to the Scottish crown. "Under his auspices," says Skene, "feudalism rapidly acquired predominance in the country, and its social state and institutions became formally assimilated to Norman forms and ideas, while the old Celtic element in her constitutional history gradually retired into the background."

During the lifetime of Alexander, David displayed the same zeal with regard to ecclesiastical foundations in the districts of Cumbria and Lothian, which formed his earldom, as animated his brother in the remaining part of the kingdom. In the year 1113 he brought Benedictine monks from Tiron in France, and settled them at Selkirk. His great work, however, was the foundation, or rather the restoration, of the bishopric of Glasgow, about the year 1115.

The pious energy of David was not satisfied by the restoration of the ancient see of Glasgow. St. Aelred of Rievaulx, his contemporary, and the biographer of St. Ninian, is lavish in his praises of the monarch's indefatigable zeal in the foundation of monasteries and erection of churches throughout the kingdom.

Toward the end of his reign, we find David granting a charter to the monastery of Deer, north-east of Aberdeen, which had been originally founded by St. Columba and placed by him under the care of his nephew Drostan. The notices contained in the Book of Deer are of particular interest, as showing that this monastery and the neighboring one of Turriff (founded by St. Comgan, in the seventh century), had continued to preserve their clerical and Celtic character down to the time of King David. "Here, if anywhere," observes Skene, "we should expect to find, according to popular notions, these Columban clergy bearing the name of Culdees; but the term *Cele De* nowhere appears in connection with them." The Book of Deer contains a number of notices of grants in favor of the monastery, some by the Earl of Buchan, and one Latin charter, as above mentioned, from King David. The charter in question declares that the clerics of Deer shall be free from all lay interference and exaction. The existence of Deer as a Celtic monastery came to an end in 1219, when it was granted by William, Earl of Buchan, to the Cistercians, who held it until the Reformation.

The Abbey of Holyrood was founded and endowed by David, in the year 1128, for canons regular of St. Augustine. The name was derived from the Black Rood, or Cross, preserved there, which, according to the legend, David had taken from between the antlers of a stag which appeared to him when hunting on the Feast of the Holy Cross. The site of the monastery is said to have been originally within the walls of Edinburgh Castle, and to have been removed, in the reign of William the Lion, to the historic spot where afterward arose the beautiful church, and the abbey and palace, with which were to be connected some of the most stirring and important events in the future history of the country.

Up to the period at which we have now arrived, we have seen the new ecclesiastical foundations of King David one by one superseding the ancient Celtic establishments, which had either entirely died out, or had become reduced to a single ecclesiastic. David did not, however, stop here in his work of reorganization, and we now find him taking active measures for the suppression of those Culdee foundations which still remained.

Robert, Bishop of St. Andrews, who, previous to his elevation to that see, had been, as we know, prior of the canons regular of Scone, established in the year 1144 a priory of the same order at St. Andrews, which he endowed with various lands, granting to it, moreover, two of the seven portions of the altar offerings (at that time in lay hands), together with the hospital of St. Andrews and its revenues. The new foundation was confirmed by Pope Lucius II in the same year. As a sort of compensation to the Culdees, whose property was thus alienated in favor of the new institute, we find David granting a charter to the prior and canons of St. Andrews, authorizing them to admit into their community the Culdees of Kilrimon, with all their possessions, provided that the latter are willing to take this step. If they refuse, those now living are to retain their property during their lives; but after their death, as many canonries are to be erected in the church of St. Andrews as there are Culdees now alive, and the whole of their possessions are to pass to the canons. In a bull dated August 30, 1147, and addressed to the Prior of St. Andrews, Pope Eugenius III deprives the Culdees of their existing right of electing the bishop of that see, and confers it upon the prior and canons—decreeing at the same time that as the Culdees die out, their places are to be filled up by canons regular. These decrees, especially that relating to the election of the bishop, appear to have been resisted by the Culdees; for we find them confirmed and renewed by subsequent popes for more than a century. By the year 1162, we find the whole of the seven portions of the altar oblations granted to the canons by Bishops Robert and Arnald (who succeeded Waltheof in 1158), on the express ground that they were living a regular life in common. Henceforth the canons regular and the Culdees formed two distinct communities; and we find Pope Honorius III, in the year 1220, issuing a bull directing his legate to inquire into a dispute between the prior and convent of St. Andrews and the bishop of that see, together with the clerics commonly called *Keledei*, regarding their respective possessions. The Culdee community now appears as the "provost and Culdees of the church of St. Mary." In course of time the name of Culdee disappeared; and we meet with it for the last time in the year 1332, when their exclusion in the episcopal election is again renewed. After this date we hear only of the provost and prebendaries of the church of St. Mary, sometimes styled St. Mary of the Rock.

It is unnecessary to dwell at the same length as we have done in the case of St. Andrews on the suppression of the remaining Culdee establishments throughout the country, such as Lochleven, Abernethy, and Dunblane. The process in every case was an identical or similar one; and the Culdee communities were one after the other superseded by, and absorbed in, the newly founded monasteries which sprang up in various parts of the kingdom.

Benedictines and Cistercians

King David, indeed, displayed even greater zeal than his predecessor in the introduction of the regular orders into Scotland. While still Earl of Cumbria, he had founded the Benedictine Abbey of Selkirk, and the priory (afterward abbey) of Jedburgh, for canons regular from Beauvais. Soon after his accession he established in the church of Dunfermline, founded by his mother St. Margaret, a community of Benedictines, consisting of an abbot and twelve monks, whom he brought from Canterbury. In 1128, the abbey of Selkirk was removed to Kelso, and sixteen years later the king founded the priory of Lesmahagow (*Ecclesia Machuti*) which was subject to Kelso. He also brought the Benedictines to Moray, establishing at Urquhart, near Elgin, a small priory which afterwards became a cell of Dunfermline. In the same district of Moray, which was by this time immediately subject to the Scottish Crown, David founded, toward the end of his reign, the monastery of Kinloss, and placed in it Cistercians from Melrose. The Cistercian Order, then at the height of its renown, was one for which the king showed a special predilection. One of the earliest Cistercian settlements was the abbey of Rievaulx in Yorkshire, founded by Robert Espec. The monks of Rievaulx, with their abbot William, had come direct from the mother house of Clairvaux; and it was from Rievaulx that King David brought monks to his abbey of Melrose, in the year 1136.

Four years later he founded the Cistercian abbey of Newbattle, near Edinburgh. Another Cistercian monastery was founded by Prince Henry, David's son, at Holmcultram in Cumberland, and colonized by monks from Melrose. Dundrennan Abbey, in Galloway, was founded by Fergus, Lord of Galloway, who brought thither monks from Rievaulx, in the year 1142.

Besides these foundations for religious men, we find convents of nuns springing up during this period in various parts of the kingdom. Among those founded by King David were the Cistercian convent of Berwick, with several nunneries dependent on it, such as Gulyne in Lothian, Trefontaney (Strafontane) in Lammermoor, and Elbottle in Haddington. The convent of Berwick was suppressed by Robert III in 1391, on account of its favoring the English cause; and its property was granted to the abbey of Dryburgh, which, like Soulseat, Whithorn, and some others, belonged to the Premonstratensian Order.

Several establishments belonging to the Military Orders also owed their foundation to King David. One of the most important was Torphichen, a church and preceptory of the Knights Hospitalers, near Bathgate. There were also several establishments of the Knight Templars, whose property, on the suppression of that Order, was granted by Pope Clement V to the Hospitalers. David likewise established at Harehope the military order of St. Lazarus of Jerusalem, which had another house at Linlithgow.

Dioceses

Among the last foundations of King David appear to have been the two bishoprics of Dunblane and Brechin. The precise date of their erection is unknown (the chartulary of Dunblane disappeared at the Reformation); but both are mentioned in a bull addressed by Pope Adrian IV to the bishops of Scotland, in 1155, two years after David's death, enjoining them to submit to Roger, Archbishop of York. With the exception of the Bishop of

Candida Casa, the Scottish prelates appear to have disregarded the Pope's commands, and to have continued to maintain the independence of their Church. Thirty years later this independence was recognized by a bull of Clement III, declaring the Scottish Church to be immediately subject to the Holy See, whose special daughter she was.

The close of David's reign thus witnessed the completion of the diocesan reorganization of the Church of Scotland, which now possessed—exclusive of the diocese of Candida Casa, which remained subject to the Archbishops of York—nine episcopal sees. Under subsequent kings we find occasional mention of seven bishops, who appear in connection with the seven earls, representing, probably, the original seven provinces of Albania. The body of seven bishops consisted, apparently, of the Bishops of St. Andrews and Glasgow and of the five sees erected by King David, the Bishops of Moray and Dunkeld being excluded.

The foundation of the various bishoprics and appointment of the bishops was followed by the erection of the cathedral chapters, to whom pertained the right of electing the bishops. In St. Andrews the community of canons regular of St. Augustine formed the chapter of the cathedral, while in Whithern it was composed of Premonstratensians. The other cathedral chapters consisted of secular canons, and were for the most part constituted on the English model. Thus the chapters of Glasgow and Dunkeld were based on the model of Salisbury, while that of Moray followed Lincoln. The first dignity in the chapters of Glasgow, Dunkeld, Aberdeen, Ross, Brechin, and Dunblane was that of dean, next to whom came the archdeacon, chancellor, precentor, and treasurer. There were two archdeaconries in the diocese of St. Andrews—viz., St. Andrews and Lothian; and Glasgow also had two, Glasgow and Teviotdale.

The different dioceses were divided into rural deaneries, of which St. Andrews had eight—Fyfe, Fotherick, Gowrie, Angus,

Mearns, Linlithgow, Haddington, and Merse. In the diocese of Glasgow there were nine—Lanark, Rutherglen, Lennox, Kyle and Cunningham, Carrick, Peebles, Teviotdale, Nithsdale, and Annandale. Aberdeen had five—Mar, Buchan, Boyne, Garioch—and Aberdeen, Moray and Dunkeld had each four: Elgin, Inverness, Strathspey, and Strathbogie in Moray; and Atholl, Angus, Stratherne, and Breadalbane in Dunkeld. The remaining dioceses— Ross, Caithness, Brechin, and Dunblane—do not appear to have been divided into deaneries.

The divine service performed in the cathedrals, like the constitution of the capitular bodies, was to a great extent modeled on the prevailing use of the English Church. The ancient Celtic ritual fell into disuse, and the Roman breviary and missal, or rather that modification of them in use in the church of Sarum, was adopted almost universally.

We find about this time the earliest notices of the holding of diocesan synods. Robert, Bishop of St. Andrews, appears to have held one at Berwick in the year 1150, at which, among other business, charters were granted conveying certain churches to the monks of Durham. It was apparently on the same occasion that Robert granted the church of Carriden to the canons of Holyrood, in a charter which was witnessed by various abbots, priors, and other dignitaries, "and by the whole Synod."

King David's family

The life of King David was not less fortunate in its domestic relations than it was beneficial to the Scottish Church and kingdom. He early lost his queen Matilda; but the grief of the monarch at the death of a partner who ever showed the warmest sympathy with his views and projects was tempered by the affection and the virtues of his only son Henry, a prince who appears to have combined in his person every quality that could endear him to his family and his country. By his marriage with Ada de Warenne, daughter of the Earl of Surrey, Henry had three sons, Malcolm and William, who afterward ascended the throne, and David, Earl of Huntingdon. He had also three daughters, Ada, Margaret, and Matilda. A severe illness which seized Henry yielded for a time to the prayers of the saintly Malachy, Archbishop of Armagh, who visited the sick prince on his return from Rome. A return of the disorder, however, carried him off in the year 1152, to the great grief, we are told, not only of his father Henry, and the whole realm, but of the neighboring kingdom of Scotland. "A brave and able soldier," St. Bernard calls him, "who walked in his father's footsteps, in justice and the love of his fellow men."

We cannot pass by without notice the striking figure of St. Waldeve, or Waltheof, David's half-brother, who stands out prominently in the religious history of this period. By her first marriage with the Earl of Northampton, Queen Matilda had two sons, of whom Simon, the elder, bore his father's name, while the younger was called after his paternal grandfather, Waltheof. Simon was brought up to the life of a soldier; Waltheof, while still in youth, embraced the religious state. In order to avoid the dignities which would probably have been conferred on him had he entered a Scottish monastery, he betook himself to the famous priory of St. Oswald's, near Pontefract. Here his reputation for learning and sanctity spread apace; and on the death of Archbishop Thurstin of York, Waltheof would have been chosen to fill the vacant see, had not King Stephen, dreading the influence that the Scottish Crown might thus acquire over the Church of England, put his veto on the election. Shortly afterward, Waltheof, in order to mark still more unmistakably his aversion to advancement and dignity, left the order of canons regular and embraced the stricter rule of the Cistercians. As a simple monk at Abbot of Rievaulx and Warden, and afterward as Abbot of Melrose (which office he held from 1148 until his death), he was a pattern of monastic zeal and fervor. It was at the instance of Waltheof that King David founded the abbey of Kinloss, and Prince Henry the priory of Holmcultram. The holy abbot was in no less favour with Malcolm IV, David's successor on the throne; and it was in great measure owing to his zeal and influence that Malcolm founded the Cistercian abbey of Cupar, and his mother Ada, Countess of Huntingdon, the convent of Haddington, for Cistercian nuns. On the death of Robert, Bishop of St. Andrews, in 1159, Walthcof was unanimously elected to succeed him; but to the persuasions of the nobles and clergy, he only replied by pointing to the spot which he had fixed on for his grave and repeating the words of Holy Scripture: "I have put off my coat; how shall I put it on? I have washed my feet; how shall I soil them again?" On August 3, 1159, he was laid to his rest.

The character of King David, whose long reign was now drawing to a close, is unanimously described by the chroniclers as one of singular generosity, uprightness, and piety. "He was," writes Aelred, "the comforter of the sorrowing, the father of the fatherless, and the ready judge of the widow. . . . I have seen him with my own eyes, when ready to go out hunting, and with his foot in the stirrup, on the point of mounting his horse, withdraw his foot, at the voice of a poor man begging, that a hearing should be given him, leave his horse and walk back into the court, and kindly and patiently hear the cause on which he had been appealed to." David's liberality in the foundation and endowment of religious institutions has not escaped censure, on the ground that he thereby prejudiced the rights of the throne; and the saying attributed to one of his successors is well known, that he was a "sore saint for the crown." Cosmo Innes, in his valuable work on *Scotland in the Middle Ages*, has met this charge in words that are worth quoting. "Even if King David," he says, "had given more of such property, I do not know that he would have deserved the character which his successor is said to have given him of being 'ane sair sanct for the crown.' However it may have become the fashion in later times to censure or ridicule this sudden and magnificent endowment of a Church, the poor natives of Scotland of the twelfth century had no cause to regret it. . . . At such a time it was undoubtedly one great step in improvement to throw a vast mass of property into the hands of that class whose duty and interest alike inculcated peace, and who had the influence and the power to command. Repose was the one thing most wanted, and the people found it under the protection of the crosier. . . . If a sovereign is to look for something more than mere revenue from royal lands, it may be doubted if they could be turned at that time more to the benefit of the country than in the administration of the religious houses."

After the death of his dearly loved son, King David gave himself with renewed fervor to the exercises of religion, doubling his alms to the poor, and confessing and communicating every Sunday. At the same time he was not unmindful of the duties of his position, and one of his last David's cares was to do all that he could to ensure the ensure the peaceful succession of his grand-children to the throne. Malcolm, the eldest son of the deceased Prince Henry, was at this time only eleven years of age, and the succession of a grandson to his grandfather—itself a novel idea to the Celtic population—was not, under these circumstances, likely to command their unquestioning adhesion. The last days of the aged monarch might well be troubled by anxious pre-sentiments of the conflict that his death would probably arouse. In order to avert as far as possible the chance of such a calamity, he caused the Earl of Fife, the head of the seven representative earls of Scotland, to conduct the youthful Malcolm through the various provinces of the kingdom, in order to secure his acknowledgment as the heir and successor to the throne.

King David breathed his last on the 24th of May 1153, leav-ing behind him the reputation of David, one of the noblest and most beneficent monarchs that ever wore the Scottish crown.

He was buried in the royal vault at Dunfermline Abbey, by the side of his parents, Malcolm and Margaret; and although never formally canonized, his memory continued for centuries to be held in veneration by the Scottish people.

Malcolm IV

David I was succeeded in the year 1153 by his grandson, Malcolm IV (styled Malcolm the Maiden), and the young king was crowned at Scone, soon after his accession, with the customary solemnities. This is the first occasion on which we hear from a contemporary chronicler of the formal coronation of a Scottish monarch. Robert, who had held the bishopric of St. Andrews, for more than a quarter of a century, died in the year 1158, and Waltheof, Abbot of Melrose, was elected to the vacant see, which, however, he refused to accept. Difficulties appear thereupon to have arisen in connection with the filling up of the vacancy, and we find William, Bishop of Moray, and Nicholas, *camerarius* of the king, proceeding to Rome the following year, and bearing to Pope Alexander III certain proposals whose tenor has not been preserved. The Pope apparently did not think it expedient to comply with them, but he received the Scottish embassy with honor, and nominated the Bishop of Moray his legate for Scotland. In the year 1160, Ernald, or Arnold, Abbot of Kelso, was elected to the vacant see, and on the 13th of November he received consecration from the papal legate in the church of St. Regulus, in the presence of King Malcolm, the bishops, abbots, and dignitaries of the land. The principal event of his short episcopate was the foundation of the cathedral of St. Andrews. Arnold died in 1162 and was succeeded by Richard, chaplain to the king, who, however, was not consecrated until Palm Sunday 1165, owing, no doubt, to the pretensions of York, which we find renewed about this time. In the year 1164, Archbishop Roger of York, in virtue of his legative powers, cited the Scottish bishops and abbots to a synod at Norham. The summons was obeyed by Ingelram, Archdeacon and Bishop-elect of Glasgow; Solomon, Dean of Glasgow; and Walter, Prior of Kelso, with some of the inferior clergy. The Scottish ecclesiastics formally protested against the claim of York and appealed to the Holy See. The result of the appeal has not come down to us, but it was evidently not unfavorable to the Scottish cause, as Ingelram, we are told, in spite of the energetic opposition of the emissaries of York, was consecrated at Rome in October 1164 by Pope Alexander himself.

King Malcolm gave many evidences of his interest in the cause of religion, and the number of monasteries and convents that were founded during his reign bear witness to the zeal that animated him, no less than his pious predecessor, in the spread of Christianity and civilization throughout his dominions. He founded the Cistercian abbey of Cupar, in Angus; a nunnery of the same order at Manuel, in Linlithgow; and a hospital at Soltre, on the borders of Lothian and Lauderdale, "for pilgrims, travelers, and poor folk." Soltre had the privilege of sanctuary, marked by a chain and cross, and still commemorated in Chain-cross Hill. Other Cistercian convents were founded at this period, at Eccles and Coldstream by Cospatrick, Earl of March; at St. Bathans (a cell of South Berwick) by Ada, Countess of Dunbar; and at Haddington by Ada, Countess of Huntingdon, mother to King Malcolm IV. There was another at Edinburgh, in St. Mary's Wynd. The Cistercian abbey of Sandale, in Cantyre, was founded by Reginald, son of Somerled, Lord of the Isles, who raised a rebellion against King Malcolm but was defeated and slain in the year 1164.

The most important foundation, however, of Malcolm's reign was that of Paisley, founded in the year 1164, for Cluniac Benedictines, by Walter Fitz-Alan, high steward of Scotland, and ancestor of the royal house of Stuart. The monks of Paisley came from the monastery of Wenlock, in Shropshire. Paisley Abbey was richly endowed by the high stewards and other powerful lords, and became one of the wealthiest and most important of the religious houses of the country.

There were at this time three orders or congregations of Benedictines proper, or black monks, in Scotland, called by the names of the French abbeys to which they traced their respective foundations. The monks of Fleury-la-Rivière had three houses in Scotland (the principal Dunfermline); the monks of Tiron six, including Kelso and Arbroath; and the monks of Cluny four, of which Paisley was the chief. The Cistercians also followed the rule of St. Benedict: their habit was white, with a black scapular.

The Benedictines come to Iona

Malcolm IV, who died on December 9, 1165, was succeeded by his brother William, surnamed "the Lion," who was crowned at Scone on Christmas Eve, 1165, and reigned for nearly fifty years.

The reign of William the Lion, like those of his predecessors, was prolific in the foundation of religious houses in Scotland. Besides the great abbey of Arbroath, the king himself founded a house of Trinitarians, or Red Friars, at Aberdeen. The Benedictine (Cluniac) abbey of St. Mary's, Lindores, was founded by Earl David, brother to the king, about the year 1178, and was confirmed by Pope Innocent III in the same year. Uchtred, Lord of Galloway, founded an abbey at Glenluce for Cistercians, whom he brought thither from Melrose. The monastery of Inchaffray was erected in 1198, for canons regular, by Gilbert, Earl of Stratherne, and his countess Matilda, in memory of Gilbert, their eldest son, who was buried there. The canons were brought from Scone. Further grants were made to the monastery by Gilbert and his wife in the year 1200.

Side by side with these new foundations, we see at this period the revival of religion in the venerable monastery from which the earliest light of Christianity had dawned upon the Pictish race. A century had elapsed since the death, in the year 1099, of Dunchad, the last of the old abbots of Iona; and thereafter, for more than fifty years, we know nothing whatever respecting the island. The title of co-arb of St. Columba was borne at this time by the abbots of Kells, in Meath, who do not, however, appear to have had any relations with Iona; nor do we find any trace of connection between the bishops of Dunkeld and the monastery. This is doubtless to be accounted for by the fact of the Western Isles being during this period under Norwegian rule. About the year 1154, the tyranny and oppression of Godred, the then King of the Isles, appears to have provoked the hostility of Thorfinn, a powerful Norwegian chief. Thorfinn made a covenant with Somerled, the Celtic ruler of Argyll, who had already succeeded in expelling the Norwegians from the mainland, to place Dubgal, Somerled's son, on the throne of the Isles; and he was accordingly acknowledged by the various chieftains as their king. In the war which followed between Godred and Somerled, a naval battle was fought, in the year 1156, resulting in the partition of the sovereignty of the Isles between the rival princes.

The island of Iona fell to Somerled, who appears to have restored the monastery, and to have placed it under Flaithbertach O'Brolchan, the Abbot of Derry. About the year 1164 a deputation of the chiefs of Iona, consisting of the Sacartmor or head priest, the Ferleighinn, or reader, the Disertach, or head of the hospice for pilgrims, and the superior of the Culdees, went to Derry in order to invite O'Brolchan to accept the abbacy. The application, however, was unsuccessful, for reasons now unknown.

Two years later, Reginal, or Ronald, Somerled's second son, succeeded his father as Lord of the Isles, and appears to have rebuilt the monastery of Iona on a larger scale. Silgrave's Catalogue mentions the *abbatia in insula*, or abbey of Iona, as occupied at this time by Culdees. The policy of Reginald, however, like that of the kings of Scotland, seems to have been to supersede the Culdees in his dominions by the regular orders of the Church; and we find, accordingly, a Benedictine monastery (probably Cluniac) founded at Iona in the year 1203. A part of the surviving Culdees doubtless amalgamated with the new community, while the remainder gradually died out.

"Thus," concludes Skene, "the old Celtic Church came to an end, leaving no vestiges behind it, save here and there the roofless walls of what had been a church, and the numerous old burying grounds to the use of which the people still cling with tenacity, and where occasionally an ancient Celtic cross tells of its former state. All else has disappeared; and the only records we have of their history are the names of the saints by whom they were founded preserved in old calendars, the fountains near the old churches bearing their names, and the village fairs of immemorial antiquity held on their day."

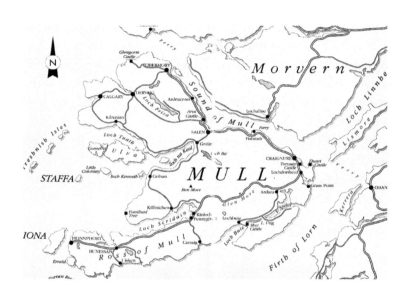

VISITING IONA

The Benedictine abbey on Iona, begun in 1203, was substantially expanded in the fifteenth century. During the Scottish Reformation of the sixteenth century, however, the abbey was abandoned and left to decay. In 1899 its then owner, the Duke of Argyll, transferred the property to a Church of Scotland trust, and in 1938 George MacLeod began the task of restoring the neglected abbey. The restoration has now continued for many decades.

Visitors to Iona today generally begin their visit from the port of Oban, on the west coast of the Scottish mainland. From Oban a vehicle ferry leaves for Craignure on the Isle of Mull.

Once on Mull, motorists can cross the island by taking the A849 road south and west to Fionnphort. A bus service also runs from Craignure to Fionnphort. Buses on Mull are run by Bowman's Tours, phone +44 (0) 1631-566-809 or visit *http://www.bowmanstours.co.uk*

A passenger-only ferry carries visitors from Fionnphort to the island of Iona.

For information on Caledonian MacBrayne ferries from Oban to Craignure, and from Fionnphort to Iona, visit *http://www.calmac.co.uk* or call 0800-066-5000 within the United Kingdom or +44 (0) 1631-566-688 in Oban.

Most visitors return to the mainland after a day visit to Iona. The following information may assist those intending to stay overnight. Note that Iona is a remote location, and all arrangements for accommodation should be confirmed in advance.

Argyll Hotel
Isle of Iona
Argyll, Scotland PA76 6SJ
+44 (0) 1681-700-334
reception@argyllhoteliona.co.uk
http://www.argyllhoteliona.co.uk

St. Columba Hotel
Isle of Iona
Argyll, Scotland PA76 6SL
+44 (0) 1681-700-304
info@stcolumba-hotel.co.uk
http://www.stcolumba-hotel.co.uk

Cnoc a' Chalmain Catholic House of Prayer
Isle of Iona
Argyll, Scotland PA76 6SP
+44 (0) 1681-700-369
mail@catholic-iona.com
http://www.catholic-iona.com

The Warden
The Iona Community
MacLeod Centre & Shop
The Abbey
Isle of Iona
Argyll, Scotland PA76 6SN
+44 (0) 1681-700-404
ionacomm@iona.org.uk
http://www.iona.org.uk